JUST AS I AM
Americans with Disabilities

To Vicky —
It's been great getting to know you.
All the best —

Ellen

Carolyn Sherer

October, 1999

VICKY,
THANKS FOR
ACCEPTING THIS AS
GIVEN. Love
Lynn

JUST AS I AM
Americans with Disabilities

Photographs by Carolyn Sherer
Text by Ellen Dossett

FOREWORD BY SENATOR ROBERT DOLE

PREFACE BY MARLEE MATLIN

A MESSAGE FROM DISABILITY ADVOCATE JUSTIN DART

AFTERWORD BY INDEPENDENT MUSEUM
PROFESSIONAL RUTH STEVENS APPELHOF

CRANE HILL
PUBLISHERS

Birmingham, Alabama
www.cranehill.com

Published by Crane Hill Publishers, www.cranehill.com
Printed in Singapore

Sherer, Carolyn.
Just as I am : Americans with disabilities / photographs by Carolyn Sherer : text by Ellen Dossett ; foreword by Robert Dole ; preface by Marlee Matlin ; a message from disability advocate Justin Dart ; afterword by museum curator and consultant Ruth Stevens Appelhof.
         p.   cm.
ISBN 1-57587-114-9
1. Handicapped—United States Biography. 2. Handicapped—United States Portraits. I. Dossett, Ellen. II. Title.
HV1552.3.S54   1999
362.4'092273—dc21
[B]   99-33976
                                                                                                   CIP

10   9   8   7   6   5   4   3   2   1

The Americans with Disabilities Act of 1990 extends to people with disabilities civil rights similar to those available on the basis of race, color, religion, national origin, and sex. It prohibits discrimination on the basis of disability in employment, state and local government services, public accommodations operated by private entities, transportation, and communications.

*J*ust As I Am: Americans with Disabilities* illustrates what I have spent my life advocating and promoting—that people with disabilities have the same desires, goals, and needs as anyone else. And given the support, skills, and opportunities needed to accomplish our goals and realize our dreams, we do just that.

Although legislation and political action have done much to further the causes of people with disabilities, there remains a mountain to climb. We must change deeply rooted attitudes. We must demolish the invisible barriers that separate us as human beings. My appeal is that we unite in a revolution to eliminate primitive practices and stereotypes, and to establish a culture that focuses the full force of science and democracy on the systematic empowerment of every person to live his or her God-given potential. No soldier ever died for a better cause.

This is a time of explosive change. We must continue to ensure that people with disabilities are not left out, and that they are valued equally and to the utmost. If we do, I think we can have a quality of life that far exceeds the imagination of Utopian fiction.

When I read the stories and see the portraits of the individuals in this book, I realize again just how lucky I am. I have the profound happiness to work with the most beautiful people in the world on the most important project in the world. I am the luckiest man alive to have the privilege of being identified as a member of the disabilities community.

Justin Dart, Jr.
National Disability Advocate

Table of Contents

viii Foreword
      Senator Robert Dole

  xi Preface
      Marlee Matlin

xiii Acknowledgments

 xvi Gallant and Gaunt Their Beauty
      A Poem by Bob Williams

   1 Introduction

Profiled Individuals

   4 John Kemp

   8 Betty Jean Smith

  10 Amelia O'Hare

  14 Carl Thompson, Jr.

  18 Matthew Sapolin

  20 Daryl Smith

  24 Bob Williams

  26 Quentin Vitalis

  30 Ronda Jarvis Ray and Joe Ray

  34 Adam Whitworth

  36 Taria Jackson

  40 Clara Link

  44 Doyle Elliott

  46 Julie Riser

  50 Ed Derrick

  54 Zachary Berish

  56 Alice Faye Love

  60 Matthew Foster

  64 Debra Finney

  66 Taylor Brasher

  70 Duane Bishop

  72 Samantha Maly

  76 Michelle Cooper

  78 Andy Morris

  82 Sepia Levy

  86 Annie Hull

  88 Donald Young

  92 Christina Kuckkahn

  96 Willie James Moore, Jr.

  98 Michael Raymond

 102 Marilyn Saviola

 106 Darron Glazier

 108 Bunni Barr

 112 Scott Harper

 116 Elaine Isemann

 118 Teresa Case

 122 Jeff Bannon

 126 Kim Sullivan

 130 Judith Heumann

 134 Tyler Marson

 136 Afterword
      Ruth Stevens Appelhof, Ph.D.

 139 Resources

Foreword

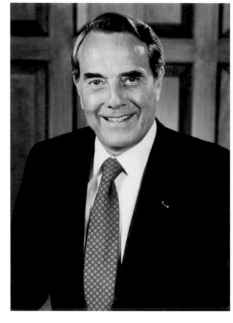

If there is one thing that unites Americans, it is our love of freedom and independence. That includes all Americans. Our nation was founded on these principles, and we continue to carve and polish these cherished ideals daily, so that all Americans have equal opportunity to live their lives freely and independently.

People living with a disability hold the same ideals, and have every right to the same opportunities to actualize their hopes and dreams. All of us have the responsibility to ensure those rights and opportunities, as the Americans with Disabilities Act of 1990 legislates. But legislation is clearly not enough. More than mandates and laws, we as a society need to see people for who they really are, understanding that all of us have contributions to make that strengthen ourselves, our communities, and our nation.

Having a disability shapes a person's life, but is not their total identity. It makes a person neither a hero nor an object of charity. Living with a disability changes one's life—not necessarily for the better or worse. It makes their life different, and different is not wrong—just different. When we can truly learn that, and let go our fears and stereotypes of people who are different from ourselves, we will have created an immeasurably better world for us all.

The growing political movement within the disabilities community can be compared to the early stages of the Civil Rights movement, and is essential for continued gains and necessary changes in our society. And while our government has responsibilities, we as individuals must also take responsibility for ourselves, our families, and our communities. We are becoming more diverse daily, and we have the opportunity to create a world in which diversity is embraced and cherished. For in reality, everybody is different in some way, and "perfection" is an illusion.

Through the pages of this book, I have the honor of introducing you to some remarkable fellow Americans. They and their families are remarkable in that they are living their lives—going to work, school, places of worship, ball games, and concerts—doing what it takes to have a good life. The increased difficulties they face daily do not prevent them from being productive Americans. What can prevent them, however, is lack of opportunity. We have done much in our country to remove the physical barriers, and legislation has helped us become aware of the ways architecture can exclude people. There is no legislation possible, however, to mandate the removal of invisible attitudinal barriers that are even more hurtful and excluding. That is our personal responsibility, and ours alone. Just as in the Civil Rights movement we had to come to know others who are different from ourselves in order to truly become friends and neighbors—to break bread together and raise our children together—so it is true for this community of people with disabilities. In order to change our beliefs, lessen our fears, abandon our prejudices, we must get to know people who may look, think, walk, and talk differently from ourselves. We must accept our responsibility to ensure that all Americans have what they need to make the most of their lives.

I have had the great fortune in my many years in public life, and now as a private citizen, to meet and come to know some of the world's great leaders. I have learned what leadership is about, and when it works and when it does not. Great leaders, whether on the world stage, in the boardroom, or around the kitchen table, have a combination of integrity, courage, character, perseverance, and will. They understand responsibility, they understand trust, and they understand what is at stake if they fail to honor that responsibility and that trust. Each of us can be a leader in this great and worthy disability rights movement, taking our place strongly and proudly beside our fellow Americans living with a disability. Our government and our society are no stronger, no fairer, no more compassionate, than each of us as we go about our daily lives. The awesome responsibility of leading others to change begins within ourselves. The responsibility is ours alone.

SENATOR ROBERT DOLE

Authors' note: Senator Dole was instrumental in the passage of the historic Americans with Disabilities Act of 1990.

Preface

Can you imagine a world in which it would not be unusual for a child in a wheelchair to be the most popular kid in school? Or for Miss America to be deaf? Or for your teacher to have cerebral palsy? Can you imagine a world where you see actors and actresses with disabilities in movies and on television so often that you don't even comment? Or a world where visible and invisible barriers were totally unacceptable—no questions asked?

We can create such a world. The individuals featured in this book are but examples of the millions of our friends and neighbors figuring out how to live their dreams, regardless of additional struggles and challenges.

As a creative artist I am particularly pleased to be a part of *Just As I Am: Americans with Disabilities*. There is nothing more significant to me than being accepted and loved for who I am. I know from personal experience the power and joy of having the opportunity to do what I love, without restriction or discrimination because I am deaf.

As a mother, I think the greatest gift I can give my child is belief in herself and confidence to try whatever she wants. I know every mother feels this way about her children, whether they have a disability or not. That's why it is so important for all of us to make sure every child, every family, has access to whatever they need to be their best, fullest, most complete selves.

And as a board member of both the Corporation for National Service and Very Special Arts, I am doubly pleased to be associated with *Just As I Am*, which had its beginning in a community service project of a group of AmeriCorps volunteers in Birmingham, Alabama. Their desire to raise the awareness of others about disabilities issues, to demonstrate the strengths and abilities of their fellow volunteers living with disabilities, and to challenge the myths and prejudices surrounding disabilities, inspired this book. This is what building community is about—bringing us all closer together in support and appreciation for each of our gifts and contributions.

By learning more about what it is like to live with a disability, by seeing up close the challenges and accomplishments of people with all kinds of differences, perhaps we can begin to create a fully inclusive world. Through the arts we have unlimited opportunities to spotlight the gifts and talents of all humans. In the words of Nelson Mandela at his 1994 Inaugural Speech:

> ". . . We ask ourselves, who am I to be brilliant, gorgeous, talented, fabulous? Actually, who are you not to be? You are a child of God. Your playing small does not serve the world. . . . We were born to make manifest the glory of God that is within us. It is not just in some of us; it is in everyone. . . ."

MARLEE MATLIN

Acknowledgments

There are so many people who have contributed their time, talents, and energy to making this book happen. First of all, kudos to Sharon Ramey, Director of the University of Alabama at Birmingham Civitan International Research Center, for the initial idea of developing a photographic exhibit featuring Alabamians with disabilities. Civitan's AmeriCorps Members of the 1994–95 class took the idea as a community project and, with the guidance of Ellen Dossett, made it a reality. The photographs, taken by Carolyn Sherer, were exhibited at the Birmingham Civil Rights Institute. The overwhelming response to the project led to the creation of *Just As I Am: Americans with Disabilities*.

To those of you who have worked silently in the background, making contacts and paving the way for others more directly involved in the project, we are deeply grateful. To Bob and Sandy Morasky, Jeanette Kelly, Denise Pesch, Mabel Dilly, Bob Williams, John Dossett, Mary Beth Romeo, Bryan and Doylene Sherer, Deb Olsen-VanCuren, Justin Catanoso, Kathy Kemp, Mary Smith, UAB's Civitan AmeriCorps Program, the Allegheny Valley School, United Cerebral Palsy of Birmingham, and Easter Seals of Washington State—thank you for your contacts, as well as editorial and other technical assistance. We could never have completed this project without your help.

We are particularly indebted to our work colleagues for the many ways they made it possible for us to concentrate our time and energies on *Just As I Am*. Nan Travis has been our constant companion, taking the lion's share of the support and making it look easy. Also, Sterling, Nikki, Brenda, Jan, Isabel, and Jane have each given of their time and attention, picking up the slack when Ellen was interviewing and writing. We want to thank, as well, Carolyn's colleagues at Birmingham Baptist Medical Center Montclair and at UAB's Department of Rehabilitation Sciences for covering for her while she was on the road photographing and in the darkroom producing the portraits for the book. Thanks to her studio mates, past and present—Virginia, Karen, Melissa, Sonja, Stuart, and Kim—who edited and critiqued her work throughout the process. No one could ask for better colleagues, and we greatly appreciate all of you.

John Kemp and his staff at Very Special Arts have been unbelievable in their tireless efforts to access the inaccessible, create the magic, and do what needed to be done way beyond the extra mile. John's infectious good humor and inordinate love of life make him an impossible guy to say "no" to. Thank you, John, for sharing your many gifts with us.

Lakeshore Foundation has truly been the "foundation" of this project—from inception through fruition. Their generous financial support has been essential throughout the process. Their unfailing and strong commitment to the disabilities community is evidenced in many ways, this project being one.

To our publisher, Ellen Sullivan, and her staff, we are so grateful for the opportunity to create *Just As I Am*. You saw the possibilities of this project and took the risk. To our fantastic design artist, Marie Weaver, thank you for the beautiful vision and creativity. And to Isie Hanson, our editor, thank you for polishing the rough edges to make these stories shine as brightly as they so richly deserve.

And there are our own families, who, during the course of this project, did without our physical presence a lot of the time, and our emotional presence even more. Thank you, Jean, Ann, and Emmy for believing in our dream enough to support us in realizing it.

Finally, to the individuals and families featured here, and those we met and spent time with who are not in the book, we owe the greatest debt of gratitude. Your willingness to share yourselves is touching. All of us who have the privilege of knowing you thank you from the bottom of our hearts.

ELLEN DOSSETT
CAROLYN SHERER

Gallant and Gaunt Their Beauty

A poem by Bob Williams

Look deep,
deep into the eyes of my people:

Caged eyes,

Peering out through the bars of their
sanitized, steel-white cribs.

Do not try to evade
their entrancing gaze
for it will not release you.

Look deep,
deep into the eyes of my people.

Look deep,
deep into the faces of my people:

Ageless but worn faces,
scarred beyond the years,

Tenuously connected to bodies,
twisted and bent
by gravity's pull
and years of lying supine.

Do not abandon those
others coldly ignore.

Look deep,
deep into the eyes of my people.

Look deep,
deep into the hearts of
my people:

Witness their horror.
Witness their pain.

Horror and pain
your spoken words alone
will never soothe.

Do not try to explain it away;
they will never believe you.

Look deep,
deep into the eyes of my people.

Look deep,
deep into the souls of
my people:

Feel their soft, entrancing
spirit.

A spirit,
which time alone
will never dim.

Look deep.
Deep into the eyes of my people.

Gallant and gaunt, their beauty.

Beauty
your spoken words can never capture.

BOB WILLIAMS IS DEPUTY ASSISTANT SECRETARY
FOR DISABILITY, AGING, AND LONG-TERM CARE
POLICY, OFFICE OF HEALTH AND HUMAN
SERVICES, WASHINGTON, D.C.

Introduction

People, first and last. This is a book about people living their lives, some ordinary and some quite extraordinary. The individuals portrayed here, and their families, face daily challenges that many of us do not, and in their stories we seek to show the ways we humans are alike—and different—regardless of our abilities.

There are as many different responses to what life brings as there are different people. In these pages you will encounter the full range of human emotions, as people just like you face their worst fears and confront their own demons while they live their lives the best they can. You will meet parents who still cannot believe their child is not the "perfect" son or daughter they dreamed of, and who agonize because that still matters. Their bravery masks their pain. Their energy and attention and care give meaning to their grief. They hold out every hope and promise, even while their hearts break with their daily reality. They search their souls for answers where there are none. They look to medical science and to God for miracles. Sometimes the miracles come; just as often they do not. But always these parents persevere, with courage and love.

You will hear from siblings who are confused and angry. They miss the attention they did not get, the childhood cut short by too much responsibility too soon. They feel guilty for being healthy, even while they resent and sometimes hate their brother or sister for not being healthy. They want to talk about how they feel, but they are so afraid of saying the wrong thing. They are sometimes fiercely protective, other times indifferent, and still other times hostile and belligerent. They are still children, nevertheless.

You will meet both children and adults who have defied every prognosis and life expectancy—people in their thirties, forties, and fifties who were not expected to survive childhood. Children who are eight, ten, or twelve who were not supposed to live beyond infancy. You will meet people who work every day, live in their own homes or apartments, have families and full lives—people whose parents were told at their birth to institutional-ize and forget them.

The people featured on these pages have agreed to share their struggles, their losses, their victories—in short, the best and worst of their lives. There is no "right" or "wrong" way to respond to a lifelong illness or disability, just different ways.

Although some of the people portrayed here express political views, this book is not a politi-cal statement. We have tried to tell these stories in the words of the people themselves, or in the words of those who know them best. In so doing we respect each individual's and family's decisions regarding care of their loved one, and their views about what is best for them, with-out regard for our own personal and political views. We ask that you, the reader, do this as well. For if we have learned anything in the course of this project, it is the value of viewing life from others' perspectives. We have heard the repeated plea of those featured here to be accepted as they are, and have learned the many ways we often, unconsciously, try to "make people over in our own image." We hope we have learned the lesson.

The human spirit is amazingly strong and resilient, and it is in that spirit that we find the most common ground and meeting place, as human beings. With each encounter and interaction we have come away feeling blessed to have been invited into the most private and personal places of the people we have come to know. It takes a large degree of courage and openness to share one's feelings about the impact of a disability on their lives and on the lives of those closest to them.

It is our hope that all of us involved in the creation of this book and you, the readers, will come a step closer to living our lives with open hearts and arms as a result of our work together. We as a society still have a long way to go in overcoming biases and beliefs about what is "able" and what is not, and we know that such internal shifts come through honest, hard, personal reflection and commitment to change.

Some of these portraits may be difficult to see, and the stories hard to read. Balancing honesty in our photographs and words with respect for the feelings of those featured here has been our mission. As we have been challenged and touched, we challenge you to open yourselves to meet some truly wonderful human beings.

ELLEN DOSSETT

CAROLYN SHERER

"There's a joyousness, appreciation, and respect for everyone, being a part of a community. When you belong you have a sense of ownership and rightfulness in your place, and others appreciate your being there too. It's where the negatives of disability, color, gender, and age go away. A perfect world would be the community where each belongs."

John Kemp profoundly lives what he speaks. He is president and CEO of Very Special Arts, an international organization providing learning opportunities through the arts for people with disabilities. Born with no arms or legs, Kemp names without hesitation his father as the most influential person in his life. "I grew

4

up under unusual circumstances. My mom died of ovarian cancer when I was fifteen months old; my older sister was five, and my little sister was three months old. And there was my dad. He was thirty-three, not well off financially, had three young kids, one with a disability. He had to figure out how to survive professionally, be the parent, get all of us going in this world, and do it in North Dakota. He gave us all this philosophy that we had every opportunity ahead of us, we just had to take advantage of it. He never accepted 'No.'"

John remembers how his dad used to talk to him constantly, not about *if* he would do things but about *how* he would do them. Once he suggested that John might want to live in an apartment building with a barbershop on the first floor. "He was thinking they could shave me and brush my hair and help me get ready for work," John says. "The message was, 'You're going to live alone. You're not going to live here, or in a group home. You're going to live independently.' He always created these expectations, and it was like, 'Of course I will. Why wouldn't I? Everyone else does.' So I just did."

In 1954, twenty-five years before the Individuals with Disabilities Education Act (IDEA), John's father put him into a regular classroom. He told the school officials to call him if there were problems, then he would come over and they would figure out a way to solve them. John remembers his dad turning down a promotion and move to Washington, D.C., because the school systems there said John would have to go to a special school. "I know he sacrificed for all of us kids," says John. "But I know that one was for me. So, he's my hero. I can hardly not cry, saying thanks to him for getting me and my two sisters launched into wonderful lives."

Today, John travels nationally and internationally, promoting the arts and the contributions to the arts by people with disabilities. He drives a car with no adaptations, using his prosthetic legs and arms. The only difference found on his computer keyboard are its dark gray keys, stained by the tapping of John's steel hooks. He writes with a pencil or pen clutched between the prongs of his left hook. Single again after eighteen years of marriage, John applauds his own independence and laughingly says he does in fact live in a condominium over the barbershop where he gets his hair cut.

John claims the depth and quality of his relationships with family, friends, and colleagues as his greatest pride. "When it's work time we work, and when it's playtime we play. That, to me, is what this world is all about," he says.

With contagious enthusiasm and enormous energy, John embraces any chance to put people at ease about disabilities. He describes the constant encounters with strangers whose curiosity about his differences forces them to ask the invariable, "So, what happened to you?"

John says, "As awful as the questions usually are, I don't criticize people. I try to get through their curiosity, thinking it will help them with other people with disabilities, and they'll see people as people."

Describing his love for his work, John says, "The arts inhabit this wonderful, limitless world, and people with disabilities can use the power of the arts to express their lives, good and bad. Through the arts we can create pride and understanding among the general public about us, and what's important to us."

Betty Jean Smith

"I wanted to major in criminal justice, but the director of the program told me you had to tote a gun, and they didn't too much want a gun in a blind person's hand," Betty Jean Smith jokes about her college days.

Blind at four from spinal meningitis, Betty knows exactly what she wants. A single mother of four children ages three to twenty-two, she says, "Even though I'm blind and have my up and down days, I've accomplished a lot, especially in taking care of my four children. It bothers me when I go, like to the doctor, and they ask if there's anyone else in the home. I know they're concerned, but so am I. I have enough sense to take care of my children."

Betty's fourteen-year-old daughter, Tamia, has spinal muscular atrophy (SMA), a genetic progressive condition that weakens the muscles. Betty provides all her physical care. Tamia, who uses a wheelchair, helps her mother look after her little brother, Raheeb, who, as Betty says, "is all over the place." Betty has neatly arranged her apartment so she can keep up with her son. She even manages to step over his toys without falling. On the dining table is a computer Betty is learning to use with the help of a telephone tutor, an AmeriCorps volunteer who is also wheelchair bound.

Betty feels strongly about how people with disabilities are treated. "People talk really loud to blind people, like we're deaf too. And as far as dating goes, sighted guys seem to be nervous around blind women, like we're different. It's like they're afraid to approach us or something. We may be blind, but we're still women."

Amelia O'Hare

Amelia O'Hare is a bright and beautiful five-year-old. She loves ballet, and keeps fairies flying in her bedroom window. She laughs infectiously at her own jokes and has long conversations with her imaginary friends.

Her parents, Catherine and Peter O'Hare, knew their lives were changed forever the day in a children's hospital when Amelia, at twenty-two months, was diagnosed with spinal muscular atrophy (SMA). A condition that causes progressive muscle weakness and wasting, Type I SMA is the most common single genetic cause of death in infants. Amelia has Type III SMA, which means she will develop scoliosis and muscle contractures, and eventually lose the ability to walk.

Suspecting that something was wrong when Amelia could not pull up at a year, and noticing that her legs and hands were shaking, Catherine and Peter read everything they could find that might give them some answers. When the pediatricians kept saying everything was fine, Catherine pressed for a referral. She recalls the pictures of the nerve patterns in SMA, and that she saw those same patterns on the screen in the hospital room the day Amelia was tested. Her heart sank as she heard the doctors talking about "denervation of the anterior horn cells." When one of the doctors came into the room and said they saw what they hoped they would not see, Catherine says, "I just grabbed Amelia and ran from the room. The doctor had told me what I already knew, but what I didn't want to know."

Peter describes standing in the parking lot of the hospital that day, holding both Catherine and Amelia. He says, "That's the day the world stopped. There was no sound, no sound at all. Just pain. I felt Catherine slipping away from me. Amelia had just been through excruciating tests. I couldn't let my family slip away. I just held them."

Catherine and Peter are like all parents. They have dreams for their child's future, "of her growing up and having her own daughter someday," says Catherine. Only now they must balance their dreams with the reality of SMA. They believe fiercely that it is their job to give Amelia all the tools she needs to be strong, feel good about herself, and focus on what she can do. They do not always agree on how to do that. Peter thinks Catherine is too easy on Amelia. Catherine thinks Peter is a drill sergeant. Peter says, "Our concerns are instinctual and natural to us, but we have to act on them without being intrusive to Amelia, without coddling or labeling her."

Practicing "tough love" is the biggest challenge they face, according to Catherine. "When your child is crying her heart out, lying on the floor, refusing to climb into bed, how do you make her do that? You know it hurts her, and you think, 'What's the harm in picking her up?' How can we expect her to do the hard things when we can't even break our bad habits?"

"The real struggle is hers, not mine, not Catherine's," Peter counters. "It's her body, her battle. No matter how much we love her, we can't fight her battles for her."

Catherine admits longing for the days of innocence when she did not know and could look at Amelia as a "normal" kid. She says, "It took me a while, and then I realized, 'Okay, she needs strength.' And for her, Peter and I both have drawn a lot of strength. I want her to have as normal a life as possible. That's why the ballet, which Amelia loves. I don't know if she can do another year or not in regular ballet. It's getting harder and harder for her."

Recently Amelia was selected to receive a wish from "Magic Moments," a private organization that grants the wishes of children with terminal illnesses or who are mobility impaired. The children are asked to make three wishes, and the organization tries to grant the first one. Amelia wanted to pet dolphins and go to Disney World, and she was granted both wishes. Amelia still talks about the dolphins. Catherine says ever since their return they have noticed a change in Amelia. "She's doing new things every day." Amelia says, "The dolphins are magic. They make me strong and they make me happy."

Peter and Catherine contemplate their life with Amelia. Catherine says, "She's already beating the odds. I am incredibly proud and in awe of her. I'm amazed at her beauty. We are blessed to have her in our lives."

"Amelia has made me slow down," Peter says. "You have to walk the world at her pace, or you deny her the ability to live her life. I'd have her no other way. That sounds crazy—I want a cure for my daughter, of course. But to know her any differently—it's impossible. Muddy Waters says it best: 'I'm gonna be all right this morning.'"

"We have a thousand bridges to cross," Peter adds. "We'll cross them one at a time. There is no road map."

Welcome to Thompson's Point of View, a neighborhood bar and Creole restaurant in Seattle where the Hallelujah wings will truly set you free. Owners Carl Thompson, Jr., and his mother, Louise, regale you with stories as they serve up southern dishes made from old family recipes. The upbeat atmosphere of the restaurant reflects Carl's attitude, despite his living with multiple sclerosis for the last thirteen years. With sparkling eyes and a warm smile, Carl, a high school football and track star, says, "I never ask, 'Why me?' When I used to make a touchdown or win a race, I never asked, 'Why me?' So why should I now? I don't feel like I've

missed out on anything, because I've been lucky to do so many things in my thirty-eight years."

Multiple sclerosis, a progressive disease, randomly attacks the central nervous system. Its wide variety of symptoms include tingling sensations, numbness, slurred speech, blurred or double vision, muscle weakness, spasticity, and even paralysis. Its progression and severity are very unpredictable. In Carl's case the disease has primarily affected his legs, weakening them to the degree that he can no longer walk.

Carl met his wife, Gail, more than five years ago at an entrepreneurial class he was teaching. "When I met her, I was done. Stick me with a fork—I was finished. She saw me; she didn't see my disabilities. She expects the most out of me. When I was too stubborn to use a wheelchair, she said she had places to go and things to do, and if I wanted to keep up with her, I'd better get me a fast chair. She doesn't let me get away with a lot of stuff. I admire and love her for that."

From a family of educators, Carl loves to speak to young people. "My proudest moments are when I've helped someone else. Everyone has something to give; everybody has worth. If you're willing to share, you have a reason for being here. I tell people what I tell myself: 'Look at the positive side. Keep your head up.' My life's taken a different path, and I've found other avenues to explore. I'm in the perfect position to influence people, young and old. Lots of people look to me for inspiration. When I keep on going, it helps them keep on going."

Carl, Sr., a retired school principal, was skeptical of his son's dream of starting a business of his own, although Louise was supportive and wanted to be a partner. "I told them they were crazy, but if that's what they really wanted, I'd get them started. And I told them I wouldn't work five minutes in the place." Louise laughs and says he's kept both promises.

Carl heads for his van, leaving the restaurant in Louise's hands as he keeps a midday doctor's appointment. One of his customers jumps up and goes to the door to help him out. Carl shakes his head good-naturedly and says, "One of my biggest challenges is getting people to understand what I can do, not what I can't do."

The Thompsons are strong and deal squarely with reality. A tight-knit family, they have stuck together, but that doesn't mean they are happy all the time. As Louise and Carl, Sr., watch their son load himself and his chair into his van, Louise's eyes become sad. "Oh, no, I will never accept that Carl has MS," she says. "You can't get used to your son being in a wheelchair. Every day of my life I say I'd gladly give it up if he could be well again."

Carl doesn't hear this; he waves and smiles at his parents as he drives off. He has places to go today.

Matthew Sapolin

Matthew Sapolin, twenty-eight, says competitive wrestling taught him about working hard. "Wrestling relies on feel, balance, and determination. It's amazing how much will has to do with it. If you want to win, you can. People didn't think a blind person could win tournaments. I loved it when I did."

Matt has been blind since he was five from retinoblastoma, a malignant tumor on the immature retina. A musician, hiker, water-skier, and philosopher, Matt is a Renaissance man who has camped and hiked across the country. "People don't realize it, but you don't have to see to know you're on the end of a thousand-foot cliff. When you're sitting with your legs over the edge, you know the floor isn't there."

With a bachelor's degree in philosophy and a master's in public administration, Matt works at the Center for Independence of the Disabled in New York, where he helps people get needed support. "I love getting inside people, learning what they're about. I'm proud when I can help somebody at work, when I achieve a goal."

Matt also cherishes family and friends. "My relationship with my girlfriend brings me joy and happiness and craziness," he says. "I feel, too, it's important to have a strong sense of right and wrong, and to fight for anything that's good.

"I think I have an advantage being blind; I'm not prejudiced by visual surroundings. Not that I don't have prejudices. I could say 'You are from the South,' so whatever judgments I have about that, I'd pass along. Beyond your accents, I don't know if you're white or black or orange or yellow-haired or dark-haired or fat or skinny. If people weren't so judgmental about things they saw and heard, the world would be a lot nicer."

Daryl Smith

Racy, raunchy, and real to the very end, Daryl Smith made one last trip outside the nursing home before he died—to Victoria's Secret. There he enjoyed the fragrances and feel of the lingerie, and planned his next visit. Perhaps his blindness was a blessing in disguise, as Daryl could not see the stares of horror as people looked at his contracted thirty-two-inch body and normal-size head.

Scarred and immobilized from a severe case of dermatomyositis since age seven, the only thing Daryl could do for himself was scoop food placed next to his head into his mouth. Yet he held onto his dreams of a normal life: "I want to become independent, to earn enough money to pay people to care for me, so I'm my own boss. I want the total right of privacy to run my own life. I want to have all the stuff that other people have like relationships—physical, romantic relationships. I'm hoping for that."

Daryl dreamed of living in a technology development house, where nurses, engineers, physical and occupational therapists, and rehabilitation and orthopedic specialists worked together. "I'd collaborate in the research and development, having all those people with imaginations in and out, being amongst them. We'd develop everything from sensors to new types of bedpans. We'd teach a blind person who couldn't walk to use an electronic wheelchair."

Sound ambitious? Consider Daryl's accomplishments. Unable to walk from age seven, blind from age seventeen, and with one year of public school, Daryl got a GED when he was twenty-seven. "I had to figure out a way to enroll in classes at the junior college. Mother was against it. She didn't want me associating with people she didn't know, afraid someone would take advantage of me." But Daryl persevered and eventually earned both a bachelor's and master's degree by taping lectures, having friends read to him, and participating in classes through telephone hookups.

Daryl's mother, Merle, cared for him almost exclusively until her death in 1995. He described the difference in his mother's and father's care: "It's almost like whiplash, a total 180-degree turn since Mother died. She was afraid for me to go out and get independent—afraid I'd get hurt. She needed me for herself too. I love Mother and she loved me, but her way of showing it was different. Daddy's way of showing it is by allowing me to be as much as I want to be—by taking risks. Actually, he never brushed my teeth until Mother died. He always did all the lifting and moving me from place to place. We're having to learn to support each other emotionally. It's really late in life for him to be learning about my physical care."

One of Daryl's proudest accomplishments was assisting in the design of the Imperium 2000, an environmental control unit for people with severe disabilities, and sharing the patent with the engineers who designed it. But after a stroke in November before he died in April of 1997, Daryl was unable to use his equipment because he could not remember numbers and names. He became isolated and depressed.

"Personal interaction is what keeps me alive, and living in this nursing home, it's gone," Daryl explains. "I can't remember new names for more than an hour. The loss of some of the things I counted on the most . . . I don't know how it works anymore. Life gets so flat. How do you end it? Maybe your body ends it. Maybe you help your body end it. I believe I can will myself to die, just like I've willed myself to do everything I've ever done in my life."

Perhaps in his death, more so than he was ever able to do in his life, Daryl realized his most passionate wish: "to come and go as I like, to have the total freedom to run my own life."

Bob Williams

Bob Williams is the Deputy Assistant Secretary for Disability, Aging, and Long-Term Care Policy at the Office of Health and Human Services in Washington, D.C. Although Bob has cerebral palsy, he has accomplished more at age forty-one than most people do in lifetimes twice as long. Early in his activist career, Bob was instrumental in writing the national legislation that supports people with disabilities in living independently rather than in institutions. He was also a key player in the passage of the Americans with Disabilities Act of 1990.

However impressive Bob's political and professional accomplishments, they are eclipsed by his enormous heart and soul, and the poetry through which he shares himself. Using a computerized voice Bob tells how he was considered "retarded" when he began school, and that one of his first teachers assured his parents that he would never learn to read.

Bob uses a motorized scooter, and has a service dog and personal attendants to assist him. His wife, Helen, often accompanies him on his numerous travels. About his work and life Bob says, "Even with all the progress we've made, I can leave a cabinet-level meeting and at the airport still be treated as if I were deaf, dumb, and blind. People see me in a scooter, with a dog, and make demeaning assumptions."

A historian, writer, policy maker, and husband, Bob lives life fiercely and compassionately. Through his honesty, and the courage to share his feelings, Bob opens the way for us to look at our hidden prejudices and fears. This is one of his many gifts and his power as a true leader.

Quentin Edmon Vitalis, age thirteen, is a lead dancer for Makah Indian tribal rituals and ceremonies. He is also a skateboarder, motorcyclist, computer expert, and football player. Diagnosed with Attention Deficit Hyperactivity Disorder (ADHD) as a young boy, Quentin sometimes has trouble in school with the teachers and the other kids. "I'm good at science, and actually school is getting better as I get older," he says. "I'm a really good linebacker—a good focuser. I look at the feet and know where they're going."

Quentin's mother, Jean, who calls him her "warrior boy," describes him as a toddler. "Quentin was like an orangutan who couldn't contain

himself. He was never idle. He required constant supervision. You simply couldn't let him out of your sight. He had absolutely no inhibitions about anything, or fear of anyone."

Kids with ADHD have a hard time with things like sitting still, concentrating, and expressing their feelings. Easily frustrated, they are often aggressive and quick-tempered. Meeting school expectations can be impossible without treatment and medication.

Jean says she was slow to catch on to Quentin's behavior. "I must have cried 'Wait!' ten billion times after he began walking," she says. "All to no avail. He couldn't wait. Accepting this fact was the most painful process of my entire life, and the guilt I feel for being so late in acknowledging his disability is enormous."

Quentin's tantrums, fights, and behavior problems in school led to getting a prescription for Ritalin, a common medication for ADHD. But Jean was so afraid of side effects and brain damage that she could not give it to him. She home-schooled him instead. Although that worked academically, Quentin was lonely and missed the other kids. Jean says that his learning the tribal dances filled the lonely void with pride and acceptance. As a result of Quentin's increased self-esteem, he eventually returned to public school.

Quentin learned the traditional dances from his brother, cousins, and grandfather, and is passing along traditions that otherwise would be lost. He can now redirect his boundless energy into beautiful, healing, celebratory dances and rituals. "Dancing makes me feel good and gets me going, kinda like listening to your favorite music, singing your favorite song—refreshing," Quentin says.

Quentin's entire family participates in his life. Jean tells of how Quentin "ran away" from a baby-sitter when he was two, ending up at his grandfather's house. "Dad was very upset," Jean says. "He declared to all of us that Quentin should not have to steal away in the dead of night to be with family. From that point on, his care has been only with family, and mostly his grandpa."

Quentin remains close to his grandfather, a respected tribal elder. "I take care of him and do things he can't do anymore," Quentin says. "I chop and bring in the wood, go to the beach with him, cut up and cook fish for him. He helps me by eating it. He teaches me a lot—tells me stories about his life when he was younger. About war—not ABC kid stuff—but about life. He really enjoys my company and likes the things I do for him. It makes him feel comfortable and loved."

Ronda Jarvis Ray and Joe Ray

"The first thing I thought when I saw Joe was, 'What a great chest.' " Ronda Jarvis describes meeting Joe Ray while they were competing at a wheelchair tennis tournament in Grand Rapids, Michigan. Ronda and Joe are both paralyzed from the waist down—she from a spinal tumor at age fourteen, and he from a car accident at age twenty.

Ronda says of the man who became her husband three years later: "I had a 'shopping list' of the person I would spend my life with, and Joe is not that. He's quiet and contemplative. But sometimes you find unexpected gifts in people. The thing I was so

attracted to in Joe is that he is very much what he appears to be—no 'toad into a prince' sort of thing."

Joe talks about getting to know Ronda and what a beautiful and talented woman she is. "You just don't run across someone like her every day," he says. "I learn something more incredible about her every day."

Both Joe and Ronda admit that sometimes it might be nice to be with someone more "able" than themselves—that they never thought they'd be with someone else with a disability. But Joe matter-of-factly says they just get creative about their daily challenges. "Sure," he says, "I'd like to be able to reach the highest kitchen cabinet. Instead, we think about where we put things ahead of time."

Joe and Ronda are both world-class athletes, having competed and won in national and international wheelchair sports. Ronda's college basketball team won five national championships, and she played on the U.S. Women's Paralympic Basketball Team, which won the silver medal in 1996. Joe is a national track-and-field finalist in the 100-meter dash. They both play tennis and water-ski. Ronda says, "Training and learning the discipline of athletics have helped me see that I can achieve just like anybody else, if I'm willing to work hard enough."

"Getting into sports after my injury helped me regain some of the pride I had lost," Joe adds. "Loss of pride is one thing a lot of people never recover from, especially when you can no longer do the most basic things for yourself without help."

Regarding the car accident that changed his life, Joe says: "I feel like I've led two lives. I was twenty when I was injured; I'm forty now. I have a good perspective on how things were going then, and if I could change things, I'd stick with sitting here on this side. If I hadn't been injured, I'd probably be in some little town somewhere, bowling on Thursday nights, drinking my beer, being a real Bubba. Opportunity is the key word here—I've had incredible opportunities as a result of my accident."

Recalling her spinal tumor diagnosis, Ronda says, "It was a lengthy, terribly difficult illness for me and my family. I think facing my mortality at such an early age was my greatest challenge, and is also one of my greatest gifts. I moved through and beyond it, and that's what has allowed me to make difficult choices, to live independently. My disability has stripped me to the bare essentials, the rawness of being human. You have to develop other aspects of yourself, beyond the physical. Joe calls it being reborn. You go through a reintegration of self, giving up this physical image of who you are. You learn your life over again in many respects."

Joe and Ronda have built a life together on a peaceful lake in the South. Their light and airy home reflects Ronda's southwest heritage. The only noticeable adaption in its design is lowered kitchen counters. The dock has a floating section, making entry into and out of the water easier. In addition to full-time "day jobs," Ronda and Joe teach adaptive water-skiing and canoeing in their nonprofit business, Spudray Adaptive Aquatics. Joe slides from his chair into his bright red Jeep Cherokee and smoothly backs the big ski boat into the lake—all in about three minutes. Ronda handles the equipment, both into and out of the boat, as they prepare for a lesson or practice their own skiing skills.

One of their greatest joys is teaching children. "There's nothing like seeing the awareness on the faces of parents who allow their child to do something as frightening as getting behind a boat and skiing," Joe says.

"To help parents see the abilities in their children and treat them no differently—not shelter and protect them or put them in a class of being less capable," adds Ronda, "that's what it's all about."

Adam Whitworth

Adam Whitworth breaks into a big smile when you enter the room. A beautiful boy, he looks the picture of health. But Adam was born with the rare VATER Association, so called because of vertebral, anal, tracheal, esophogeal, and renal problems. Adam's esophagus didn't meet his stomach but grew into his trachea. He had curvature of the spine and several malformed vertebrae. He weighed only three and a half pounds at birth, and the umbilical cord, which was twisted around itself, was very small. Adam's mother, Tracie, says, "This child is many miracles."

Despite a grim prognosis, Adam has defied the odds. With several surgeries successfully behind him, he continues to improve. Tracie is convinced that Adam's status is due to the prayers of many believers in her church and neighboring churches. Her husband, Barry, is one of eleven Whitworth children who grew up on the mountain where they still live. When word got out that a Whitworth baby was born with health problems, people flooded to the hospital to pray for him. Instead of being in the hospital the predicted eight months, Adam came home in one month.

For a young mother who manages a four-year-old son, a fifteen-month-old son with serious health problems, and a family business, Tracie exudes a quiet peacefulness. Many nights, since Adam needs breathing treatments to relieve his severe asthma, she gets just two hours of sleep. Yet she says, "When you have a child with a disability, it's not a curse; it's a blessing. It might take a while to figure out the blessing, but it's there. This child has had such an effect, not just on our family, but on this whole community."

"It's just a wheelchair, ma'am. I just can't walk. I'm not any different from anyone else. God made us all in His image, so at some time God was in a wheelchair."

Taria Jackson responds to a woman staring at her in Wal-Mart recently. Born with spina bifida, which is a hole in the spine that causes paralysis, Taria has been in and out of hospitals dozens of times in her short life of seven years. She has survived operations and infections. As she enters the second grade this year, Taria is finally enjoying better health.

She also is included now in regular classes at her school, where she is thriving. Her mother, Dorsann, says, "In her special education class there

were only six or seven kids, and they babied them so much. Now she's in a class with twenty other kids, and she's learning and growing. Every day she comes home with new words and a new sense of independence."

"I like school," Taria says. I like my therapist and my teacher. I like to play at PE, on the playground, and on the car-tire swing. We swing real high and act like we're going up to the sky. I like to play with the dollhouse, and I like to color, especially a rainbow. I want people to treat me nice; I don't like it when people stare at me."

Dorsann adds, "At first it was hard for me to accept the fact that Taria had a disability, and seeing people look at her as if she were so different. We've both grown a lot in terms of acceptance. People look at her in pity. She is not pitiful."

Outgoing and friendly, Taria "knows everybody in town," her mother says. "She invites people over—tells them we're having a party. This summer we were planning to go to Disney World. I got a call from another little girl's mother, asking what she needed to pack for her daughter's trip to Disney World. Taria had asked her friend to go along, and I had to tell the little girl's mother we didn't have room for two wheelchairs in our van."

Dorsann describes Taria as an "old soul," who seems to understand life beyond her years. She tells how Taria consoles her when things are bad, like when she is really sick. "She'll say, 'It's gonna get better, Mommy. Stop crying,' " Dorsann says.

"If I could change anything in the world, I'd be able to walk," Taria comments. "Then I could go play when I want to, and walk to my grandmother's house and walk to church with her, so she wouldn't have to carry me. I'd be able to go to the bathroom by myself, and wash dishes, and dust off the furniture while Mom is vacuuming. I'd also have my own nose ring in my nose."

Dorsann's desire for her daughter is this: "Just give Taria a chance. Don't judge the book by its cover. I want people to see what I see, which is to see everybody the same. I see her as a child. I wish people would think before they speak, and if they don't know, ask. I try to treat every day as a normal day, as if she's going to live a normal, productive life."

As her mother talks, Taria looks at her Minnie Mouse wristwatch and says, "There's nothing for me here. I want to live in Orlando!"

Clara Link

Visitors at the Links's home are likely to be met at the door with the flash of a camera. Twenty-six-year-old Clara Link, the official photographer for the National Down Syndrome Conference in Miami in 1997, loves taking pictures. She also loves to ski and swim; one of her goals is to be a lifeguard.

Clara's mother, Yvonne, talks about being a widow with a young child with Down syndrome. "Being an Asian woman living in this country and trying to do everything on my own—I just did what I had to do to survive and bring up my two kids. I'm happy to be living in America, because it really doesn't matter whether you have a disability or are a minority. If you are willing to work, the opportunities are limitless."

And the Links have seized their opportunities for success. Clara's older brother is a Stanford University graduate and a U.S. Naval officer. Clara graduated from high school and is certified in CPR and first aid. She volunteers as a lifeguard assistant and in the pediatric ward at Madigan Medical Center. Yvonne went to school after her husband's death in 1980 and earned a master's degree in counseling. She uses her knowledge and training to support other Asian families in speaking up for their children with disabilities, helping them receive their legal benefits. "If parents don't know their children's rights, they're not going to ask for them," Yvonne explains.

As Yvonne talks, Clara brings out albums of photos she has taken, and ribbons and awards she has won in athletic competitions. A member of the Ski Hawks, a racing team, she participates in Ski-for-All activities in the winter. Abundant photographs and mementos chronicle Clara's accomplishments through the years, and she loves to show them off.

Clara's life is wide. In addition to her volunteer work, Clara is a consultant with Pierce County Human Services, taking photographs for special occasions, official publications, and exhibits. Clara attends church, where she has a group of friends her mother does not know. Says Yvonne, "I take her and pick her up, but it is a time for her to be without me. It gives us both time to be alone, which we can really use." Fun-loving and extroverted, Clara often goes to movies and out to eat with friends.

Yvonne recalls the conversation she and her husband had with the pediatrician right after Clara was diagnosed with Down syndrome. "He told us our options were to give her up, put her in an institution, or keep her at home and love her. Of course, there was no option but to bring her home. My goal in life is for Clara to have the opportunity and chance to try whatever she wants to do, just like her older brother. I want her to be as independent of me as possible, so that when I'm not here, she can make it without me. I hope her brother will volunteer to be responsible for her, but I don't want to ask him.

"It has not always been easy, of course. Clara has felt hurt, particularly when she has not been able to get a job just because she has Down syndrome. She passed the training for baby-sitting, for example, but when the mothers find out she has Down syndrome they won't call her. The key to Clara's success has always been to find someone who believes in her, and who will give her a chance.

"If I could change anything about the public, I'd have people be more aware and open-minded. Because someone looks different, that doesn't mean their desires are different."

Doyle Elliott

Doyle Elliott has lived the last two of his ninety years in an Alabama nursing home, ever since a stroke left him unable to care for himself. Still handsome, with piercing blue eyes, Doyle has always been a strong and outspoken man. Today he speaks few intelligible words and can no longer walk. His daughter, Doylene Sherer, goes to the nursing home daily to see that he is cared for.

"It was a hard decision to bring him here—definitely hard," Doylene says. "But he had become completely dependent, and his wife wasn't able to take care of him."

Doyle was seriously injured by a tornado when he was nine. His mother was killed, and his sister and two brothers were also injured. He was fourteen when his father died, and he dropped out of school to work and take care of the younger children. Throughout his life Doyle followed work, from the coal mines in West Virginia to oil fields in Oklahoma to automobile plants in Michigan. According to his sister, Wilma Elliott, "he'd build up a nest egg and come back home to farm, but you can't make a living farming."

Doylene remembers how her father was before his stroke. "He could be the kindest, sweetest big fellow in the world, and in thirty seconds he'd curse you out if you crossed him. But he'd also give you the shirt off his back. It is hard to see him as he is today—a man who always spoke his mind, almost unable to speak at all."

Still, when Doylene's husband, Bryan, teases Doyle about flirting with the nurses, Doyle grins and responds with one of his few remaining words, "sonsabitch."

Twelve-year-old Julie Riser loves to sing in the children's choir at her church. Julie gets her book, holds it like the other kids, and turns the pages when they do. But when the other children sing, Julie makes her own "joyful noise."

The Risers's church exemplifies the many positive experiences they have had with Julie, who was born with cytomegalovirus (CMV), a condition that causes multiple handicaps, including speech difficulties. Before her last orthopedic surgery, Julie needed a walker to get around, but now she walks on her own. Julie's mother, Margaret, says the choir room used to be on the second floor of the building, and they had to

walk outside and up two flights of stairs to get there. One day they arrived for choir practice to find that the choir room had been moved downstairs—to accommodate Julie.

In addition to choir and music, Julie loves horseback riding, swimming, canoeing, school, and anything that includes being around other people. She enjoys having someone read to her along with her sisters, Katherine and Elizabeth. Although Katherine is a year younger than Julie she has the role of the older sister and is protective. Just the same, Katherine says, "I wish Julie could talk, so she wouldn't have to pull my hair to get my attention." Julie uses a communication computer and limited sign language to make her thoughts and wishes known.

Julie goes to school in her neighborhood, where she attends some classes with other children with disabilities and some regular classes. According to her mother, "A lot of Julie's educational needs are around daily living—like going to the bathroom, dressing herself, combing her hair. It wouldn't be appropriate for her to go to academic classes that would distract her from doing what she is trying to do. It wouldn't be fair to her or the other kids."

Julie's physician parents, Margaret and Tom, plan to keep Julie in their home as long as possible. They think a high-quality group home setting will eventually be good for Julie, because she thrives on being with other people. "We think as she gets older, and the other girls are gone from home, the group home will be best for Julie," says her mother.

Margaret says her family has been touched by the kindness of others. She tells of a recent skiing vacation when the hotel bellhop brought Julie a very large-wheeled chair and a little sled. "He just thought that would be nice for Julie while we were there," says Margaret. "I think maybe that's been one of the pluses—we've been able to see people's small touches of kindness that we wouldn't necessarily know about, as a result of Julie's handicap."

Families respond to having a child with a severe disability in many different ways—as many ways as there are families. Margaret says, "You think you have your life all mapped out. You get an education, get married, have a family—and then you just take a different route. You deal with the hand life gives you."

Eleven-year-old Katherine comments with a child's honesty, "If I could change anything, I'd just make Julie into a normal person."

Her mother responds with a smile, "Yeah, but then she might not be Julie."

Ed Derrick recalls that when he was a teenager trying to date native girls, their mothers would run him away because of his blond hair and blue eyes. "They didn't believe I was Indian." Although mostly bald now, Ed still has those sky-blue eyes, a gift from his Norwegian grandfather.

Raised by his Native American grandmother, Ed tries to live by what he learned at her side—respect for nature, and a love of hunting and fishing. "I believe in the Great Spirit of God. My accident got me where I am, and I believe I'm here for a purpose. Life is round, and everything that goes 'round, comes 'round."

When the truck Ed was riding in on his way to a construction job nine

years ago was broadsided, he assisted the other guys with first aid. It was not until he was x-rayed at the hospital that he realized his back was broken. About to enter a drug and alcohol rehabilitation program at the time of the accident, Ed went on into treatment. Because of his drug abuse history, he still won't take prescription drugs for his chronic back pain. "I'm afraid to," he says.

One of the hardest things for Ed was the effect of his injury on his relationship with his daughter, then eighteen months old. " I used to come home from work, swoop her into my arms and play with her," he says. "After the injury, I'd try to hold her and get down on the floor and play with her, and we'd both end up crying—I from pain and she from thinking she'd hurt me. I used to lift 200 pounds; now I can pick up 30. I used to walk 10 miles to go hunting; now I can't walk to the grocery store."

It has been difficult, too, that sometimes friends ask him if he has just gotten old and lazy. "They don't understand about this pain, and that hurts me," Ed says.

After the accident, Ed received drafting training through workmen's compensation insurance. Along with the technical skills he learned, Ed says the education was significant for him in other ways as well. "I'm proud of the influence on my daughter, teaching her by example that school and education are important. I've learned the computer skills necessary to design home modifications for people with disabilities. I know that I improve their quality of life through their home changes."

In addition to the physical modifications he designs for people's homes, Ed would like to change some cultural differences he has noticed. "I had a client who came here from an Asian country. He was about to take his son, who had a head injury, into the hills and either euthanize him or the two of them [would] live there in exile, because of the stigma and difficulties of life in their country. Instead, he saved his money, got visas, and brought his family to the United States. We were able to help that family, by the grace of God and through grant support of Easter Seals. I'd like to see that help available to people in their own countries."

A quiet, gentle bear of a man who collects antique fly rods and old books, Ed has a clear message for people who are not disabled. "Look at a person with a disability and realize that at any second it could be you. Think of how you would want to be treated—with love, respect, and kindness—and treat that person like that."

Zachary Berish

"Anybody who has had a catastrophic event and says they never ask 'Why?' is full of it. You ask 'Why?' again and again and again. 'What did we do that was so bad?' Yet you know in your mind that you haven't done anything."

Daphne Berish holds her son, Zachary, who has anencephaly (an undeveloped brain). He is blind and deaf and cannot support his body in any way. He seems unaware of his surroundings, except for an occasional groan when he may feel discomfort. Expected to survive only a few months, Zach is now eight. He lives in a residential center in central Pennsylvania close to his parents, Daphne and John, and his six-year-old twin sisters.

Zach lived at home for eight months. Daphne, a neonatal intensive care nurse, thought, "I'm a nurse. I should be able to fix anything." But she couldn't fix her child. Deciding to put him in a care center was excruciating. John admits he held out hope. "Daphne tried to convince me he was never going to be fine, and I kept dreaming he was." Finally Daphne took Zach to the care center. "It's a wonderful place. Still, it's not our home," she says.

Every day Zach goes to school, where he gets physical therapy and interacts with other children and his teachers. Daphne says, "He's accomplished so much more than was ever expected. I think, more than anything else, as much as we love him, we were the messengers for him. He is here for a reason."

The Berishes conclude their weekly visit with Zach. The twins climb all over him while John and Daphne referee. As they prepare to leave, Daphne sits on the floor and rocks Zachary, singing to him. She says sometimes he turns toward her, or gets real still around the twins, and she thinks he might know them.

Alice Faye Love

As you listen to Alice Faye Love, you wouldn't know she has Dissociative Identity Disorder, formerly called multiple personality disorder (MPD). A person with MPD has two or more distinct "alter" personalities, who have different histories, self-images, and identities than the host, or dominant, personality. Alice Faye identifies several "alter" selves, who may emerge when she is stressed. There's "Alice in Wonderland," who is optimistic, helpful, and thoughtful, but also fragile and needy. Her "James Dean" identity, the tough, cigarette-smoking protector, comes to the aid of Alice. There are other unnamed personalities, such as the enraged one who usually causes Alice Faye physical harm by provoking others. "Barbie" uses sexuality to get what she wants.

The Alice Faye speaking today says: "I am Alice Faye Love, an international multimedia performance artist. Raised between my upper-crust father and stepmother lawyers; my working class, pink-collar mother; and my dirt-farming grandparents in Clay County, I had a broad cultural experience growing up."

Knowing what brings on her dissociation, Alice Faye has learned to cope by removing herself from society a lot of the time. While this strategy usually works in controlling the MPD, it also means she lives an isolated, lonely life. And working for, or even with, anyone else is pretty much out of the picture.

Alice Faye relies on several different medications to help manage her illness. Depending on what is going on in her life, she may take an antidepressant, an anti-anxiety, and something to help her sleep. She says that often she can sleep only three to four hours a night.

Describing her MPD, Alice Faye says, "I have a 'hidden disability,' and society is not kind to people like me. It'd be much better for me if I was blind, or in a wheelchair. Then society would be more accepting. One of my therapists told me if I moved outside the South—'the cotton curtain'—to a large city, many of my problems might resolve themselves. But you can't just pick up and move on disability income. Try living on five hundred dollars a month. I tell people I live on a trust fund—I trust each month that the check is coming in. So I've coped with my disability by becoming an artist.

"In 1980 I was diagnosed with stage-three ovarian cancer and given six months to live. As you can see, I'm still alive, but at the time I went into massive grief and had to ask myself, 'If I'm only going to live six months, what will I do with my life?' I moved to Tennessee to contemplate my belly button, and some female artists took me to see Judy Chicago's *Dinner Party*, which opened the door for me. Art had always been a hobby with me, but then art became a way of expressing pain—things I couldn't really verbalize. The theory is if you can draw it, write it, speak it, it loses power over you.

"You want to know what's the hardest thing for me?" Her eyes intensify. "Living. Feeling like I don't fit in, the isolation that comes from that. Living in a society that's not kind, with a disease that you never know when it will rear its head again. Living with the fear of abandonment, thinking, 'When they see my disability, they're not gonna love me.'

"I'm not that different from anybody else," Alice Faye continues. "My pride gets bruised a lot. But so does everyone else's. I'm trying to look for things that make us more alike than different, because I'm tired of being the only one dancing in 4/4 time to a waltz."

Matthew Foster

Fifteen-year-old Matthew Foster says without hesitation, "I want people to know I'm great. I love myself. I don't like people to make fun of me. It makes me feel bad. I'm not making fun of them. I have Down syndrome and I'm black. You can't say the "n" word—that's bad."

Matthew is fully included in the ninth grade of his high school, which means he goes to classes with everyone else. His family moved to their current neighborhood precisely for the school system, which has the best reputation in special education. Matthew, who has mild mental retardation, likes Ms. Caffey's English class best. "They don't make fun of me," he says. "They're nice. And sometimes Ms. Caffey gives us donuts." Matthew is a member of the art club and plans to go out for basketball this year. He likes high school because he feels grown up there.

Susan, Matthew's mother, remembers when she and her husband, Mike, learned of Matthew's diagnosis shortly after his birth. "I was totally devastated. But Mike was like 'Yeah—this is what he is, and if it's Down syndrome, that's what it is.' Mike has a nephew with Down syndrome, so he knew even better than I did what it meant. And it really, really didn't matter to Mike. I remember his writing in Matthew's baby book about his plans for them together—taking him fishing, camping—talking about having the son he'd always wanted.

"I'll never forget being at an early intervention conference when Matthew was eight or nine, when a woman read a poem that said something like, 'Let me love you for who you are, but let me grieve for who you might have been.' Well, that's wrong. Matthew, from the top of his hair to his toenails, is who he was meant to be, and he's absolutely perfect in every cell of his body just as he is. He is different, but he is not 'chosen,' and he is not 'punished.' He is just different."

Matthew has hopes and dreams for the future. "I want a wife, children," he says. "I want to visit my brother, Teddy, and sister, Courtney. My mom and dad are going to build me my own house in our backyard, so I'll have a place to live when they're gone."

Like most fifteen-year-olds, Matthew counts his friends among the most important things in his life. Planning his next birthday party, he says, "We'll have a slumber party, watch TV, eat pizza, sleep in sleeping bags. I'll invite my friends Mack, Jonathon, and Curt."

Matthew proudly shares that he made five hundred dollars last summer working at the park—and put it in the bank. He remembers his family's vacation. "We went to Six Flags in Texas this summer. My favorite was the Runaway Mine Train, where you go up and down. Teddy was a hero, 'cause he caught my dad's hat when it blew off his head on the ride."

Susan listens to her son, then says, "If I could change anything about this world, I'd wipe away all stereotypes, all misconceived notions about Down syndrome. I'd start from a clean slate. I'd have everybody—everyone—accepted for exactly who they are."

She quotes from a poem Matthew wrote about wanting a twin. He would teach his twin basketball and how to use his locker. Matthew ended the poem with, "It could happen . . . in my dreams."

Debra Finney

The only thing Debra Finney likes more than being photographed is shooting her own photos. Her mother, Mazell Parsons, says she will "break the bank buying film if you let her."

Sitting in the garden at United Cerebral Palsy, Debra proudly talks about her job there. She tends the garden, cleans the kitchens, and washes the children's classroom toys. She also enjoys assisting fellow workers with daily tasks they cannot do on their own.

Debra, age forty-two, has Down syndrome. She has lived in a group home since the mid-seventies, when she left a state institution for people with mental retardation and developmental disabilities. Mazel talks about how hard it was to put Debra in the institution at age five. "I was a single, working mother, with three other children, and Debra required more attention than the sitters could provide."

Even though she does not read, and her speech is hard to understand, Debra is described by her friends as the life of the party and full of joy. She is also sensitive to others' feelings and wants to make them feel better when they are down. Debra loves to sing and dance, and has lots of boyfriends.

Not unlike many people with Down syndrome, Debra's physical aging process is somewhat accelerated. Although still energetic and active, she gets fatigued more quickly than before. Debra's mother says the one thing she cannot stand is people teasing her daughter and others with disabilities. "I don't know if they think they're doing her a favor or what. But I really don't like that. Debbie is a sweet-hearted person. She loves life and never meets a stranger."

Taylor Brasher

"The hardest thing for me is that Taylor is nonverbal, and that I'm not able to reason with him. He gets real frustrated when he doesn't understand, and that's when he goes to banging and knocking things around, being destructive."

Cathy Brasher talks about her twelve-year-old son, Taylor, who has Angelman's Syndrome. Also called "Happy Puppet's Syndrome," it can cause severe to profound mental retardation. Being nonverbal, Taylor communicates with gestures, sounds, and facial expressions. "We tried to teach him sign language when he was younger," Cathy says, "But his eye-hand coordination is just so poor he couldn't do it. He pretty much feeds himself but can't dress himself. He's potty trained.

"Another challenge is that he sleeps only five to six hours a night," Cathy says. "I'll put him in bed with me and turn the TV on, so I can get some sleep. When he's in his room at night, if the doors aren't locked, he'll get out and ransack the house. We use a chain lock, so he can open the door and see that everybody's there, and he'll eventually settle down."

A seventh-grader at Moody Middle School, Taylor has his own individual aide. Included in nonacademic classes such as art and physical education, and otherwise in special education classes, he likes going to school. And he loves riding the school bus.

Taylor also loves to swim. Cathy put a pool in the backyard so he could swim every day. He watches videos and looks at magazines, feeling the texture of the paper. "He likes to aggravate our poor dog, Maggie," his mom says. "They seem to understand each other. No matter what Taylor does to Maggie, she never once has snapped at him."

Looking out the window at her brother and nephews working on a car while her parents entertain Taylor in the living room, Cathy talks about her family. "I think Taylor's brother and sister will be better people because of having Taylor in our home—because of having to protect and care for somebody who can't protect himself. I think they have a better understanding about other people with disabilities.

"Just because someone has a disability doesn't mean they don't have feelings and don't know if they're being treated good or bad, because they do. Taylor's just like anybody else. He has his wants, his likes, and his dislikes. When he's ignored, that's when he gets up in people's faces and gets aggressive. I think Taylor is sensitive too. Everybody's always going in and out, and he wants to go too. He'll stay out on that glider from daylight to dark, if you'll let him, watching the traffic and what's going on.

"What do I see his future like? I don't know—he's not ever going to be independent. I figure he'll be somewhere where he can have care. Sometimes I can see myself putting him into a group home, sometimes I can't—but never in an institution. The ideal thing would be to bring someone in, but we just can't afford that.

"His daddy's remarried, and they have a little boy with Down syndrome. That's pretty much crushed his world—having another child with a disability. I think it's real confusing for Lindsay, my daughter. She probably has a lot more questions than she cares to ask. She spends a lot of time with both of them—Taylor and the other baby. She says she's not having any kids.

"Mostly I want people to be more educated about disabilities," Cathy concludes, "to be more understanding about Taylor's language. Instead of being so scared and back-offish, to be more willing to talk to him, to acknowledge that he is there. A lot of people seem to think that when you have a mental disability, you're just not there. But he is, and he'll let you know, 'Hey, I'm here too—hello.'"

Duane Bishop

"When I came home after the stroke," says Duane Bishop, "I asked, 'Quay, how can you love me? I'm defective.' She said, 'For better or for worse.' "

Duane had a stroke at forty-four. A self-professed workaholic, he managed four plumbing supply stores, was his company's top salesman, and was a volunteer fireman and EMT. Learning to do everything over again has not been easy. Duane runs his own business now, selling products to modify homes for people with disabilities. "I can't think of a grander thing to be doing. I build with empathy. I can't do anything about your disability, but I can help you in your home. We all heal better in our homes."

Duane and Quay spend much time organizing stroke support groups. "People look at me and can't see that I had a stroke. But when I start talking, stutter and say something stupid, they see I'm just like them." Quay says to family members of people who have had strokes, "Don't give up on them. Sometimes I had to *make* Duane take care of himself, because he wouldn't do it on his own." Duane laughs and says he has leaned on Quay so much she is four inches shorter than she was before.

Duane and Quay's two daughters are also active in their father's recovery. Duane's eyes fill with tears as he talks about the night his sixteen-year-old got permission from her volleyball coach to leave the game so she could walk her dad into the gym. And twenty-one-year-old Kim says of the changes she sees in her father, "He's so much happier now, because he knows he's helping. He's out there to help people."

Samantha Maly

Samantha and Jessica Maly are identical eighteen-month-old twins. They toddle around the house, picking up whatever is not nailed down. Their four-year-old sister, Jordan, runs in and out of the room, tolerating their attacks on her and her things.

Their parents, Scott and Michelle, talk about Samantha. "A few minutes after the twins were born a nurse came in and said to us, 'Baby "A" has some birth deformities.' We said, 'Like what?' She responded, 'Oh, one leg is short and she's missing some fingers.' We asked, 'Well, but is she okay?' From the beginning, it was like the deformities were secondary, as long as everything else was fine and she was healthy and normal otherwise.

"Within hours they did a lot of tests, and they told us she had missing limb syndrome, or Proximal Femoral Focal Deficiency (PFFD). The femur either doesn't grow at all or is much smaller than normal, so that her left leg and right arm are shorter and malformed. She's already had two surgeries on her hand, to fuse two fingers and remove an extra finger growing from one knuckle. Eventually they will surgically reposition her left leg, turning it 180 degrees so it will face backwards and the heel will work like the knee, making it possible for her to use that leg with a prosthesis."

Samantha gets around with a sort of "Rambo"-like scoot, keeping up just fine with her sisters and all the action of the household. Scott and Michelle are determined that Sam will have whatever she needs to reach her goals and that she will not be treated differently from the other girls. "We have to make sure we're not doing everything for her, so that she learns to do things for herself. In the beginning, her grandparents sort of felt sorry for her and wanted to give her special treatment. But the more they're around her and see what she can do for herself, the more at ease they are," says Scott.

As pharmacists, Scott and Michelle say they have seen so many situations that are a hundred times worse. "Of course we were shocked at first about Sam," Scott says. I prayed, 'God, if you took my left leg and my fingers and gave them to her, I'd be happy. Can you do that?' You know I'd do that in a heartbeat. But Sam's amazing. She's a little trooper. Of the twins, she has the stronger, more outgoing personality, and I think she's the better one to deal with this—she's very spunky."

Sam's surgeries have been at the Scottish Rites Hospital in Atlanta, and Scott and Michelle cannot say enough about the care she gets there. "Not only are the medical people great, but we've been able to meet some other families with kids who have the same condition Sam has. We saw one little girl who's had the leg surgery, and she skates now. That's so wonderful."

Michelle says this reinforces their decision to seek other opinions before deciding about Sam's treatment. "We were told at the first hospital, when Sam was only a few weeks old, that we should have both limbs amputated. My advice to other parents is: 'Always, always do your homework, and seek a second opinion before making any major decisions.'"

The only indication that big sister Jordan notices anything different about Samantha is that one day she was looking at her sister's hand and said, "Mommy, it's broken." Michelle responded, "No, Honey, it's not broken. That's the way God made it."

Michelle Cooper

If you ask Michelle Cooper what she would like to try, she will grin and say, "Sky dive." Her husband, Wayne, rolls his eyes and says, "She's just crazy enough to try it too."

Michelle's approach to life is, "If you want to do something, find a way." She spent ten years getting an accounting degree, then almost two years looking for her first paying job.

At thirty-one, Michelle is ten years beyond the life expectancy given her when she was seventeen. She was diagnosed with Freidrich's ataxia, a progressive neuromuscular disease that causes muscle weakness, loss of sensation, and accompanying conditions such as heart disease, diabetes, and hearing and vision loss. Michelle and Wayne see the gradual decline in her strength and stamina, yet they live their lives with zest and good humor.

On the days Michelle works as consumer coordinator at the Civitan International Research Center in Birmingham, Alabama, she and Wayne rise before four. Wayne bathes and dresses Michelle, drives her forty miles to work, then drives to his job sixty miles in the other direction. During Michelle's reign as 1998 Ms. Wheelchair Alabama, Wayne helped her shop, styled her hair, and fixed her face before each appearance. Not bad for a guy who otherwise works on equipment in a machine shop.

Michelle passionately encourages all people to see abilities rather than limitations, and to allow people with disabilities the same opportunities as everyone else. "Don't ignore me," she says. "Don't pretend you can't see me. Don't act like you want me to get out of the way. Remember, everyone is a person with a heart, a mind, and feelings. Be sensitive, and keep that sensitivity in your mind, your heart, your thoughts."

Andy Morris

Andy Morris zooms into the front yard on his newest Kawasaki Mule, a small off-road utility vehicle. Andy uses his Mule to get around in the rural community where he lives with his parents, Jan and Ricky Morris. He has just returned from checking on the Full Gospel Tabernacle, where he is an active member.

Twenty-two-year-old Andy was born with Prader-Willi syndrome, a genetic disorder that causes poor muscle tone, mental retardation or learning disabilities, speech deficits, incomplete sexual development, and obsessive behaviors. By far the most life-threatening effect of Prader-Willi syndrome is a malfunction of the hypothalamus, the part of the brain that controls hunger and satiation. As a result, individuals with this disorder never feel they have satisfied their hunger and typically develop food obsessions that result in severe obesity.

Most attempts at treating Prader-Willi syndrome, such as taking appetite suppressants and controlling access to food, are not very successful. What usually happens is the person learns more clever and devious ways to get food, such as stealing it or raiding garbage cans.

Treatments work best in restrictive and controlled settings. Because of this, Andy's family has chosen to do what they can at home, trying to provide him with as normal a life as possible. When he is in the house alone the refrigerator remains locked, and Andy's mother keeps healthy foods available.

Still, at 5 feet, 4 inches tall, Andy weighs about 370 pounds. It is difficult for him to walk far, and until he recently underwent corrective surgery he could not sleep lying down. Now, with the help of breathing equipment, Andy sleeps in his bed again, rather than sitting up in an easy chair all night.

Since he completed high school, Andy has worked part-time in a nearby workshop, where he does assembly tasks for local business and industries. He is involved in his community, assisting the high school baseball and basketball trainers.

Andy talks with a grin about his participation in two upcoming weddings. He has already told one of the brides that he will not wear a tuxedo. "Nope," he says. "Derrick [the groom] said he ain't wearing one, so if he don't wear one, I don't have to." When Andy's mom asks him what they are wearing, he answers with a laugh, "Blue jeans."

Jan says, "Parents and friends and grandparents have to include the person with a disability. Not that we've done everything right, but we've always tried to include Andy in our life and in our circle of friends and family. Now all these kids are growing up, and they're doing the same thing. You know, the circle is broadening."

Andy loves to 'coon hunt with his daddy and his friends. During hunting season they take their dogs and go out one or two nights a week. Andy enjoys being with the other guys, "just hanging out and watching and listening to the dogs run and bark."

Usually somewhat childlike and jovial, Andy turns serious when asked about the hardest thing he has ever faced. Hesitating, looking at his mom for support, he quietly says, "When people laugh."

Jan elaborates, "It's hard when people stare and make comments. Not kids, really, 'cause they're just kids. But you can tell what kids hear from their parents by the way they act toward Andy. Not long ago at the mall some kids were staring and laughing and making fun of Andy, and I said to them, 'Hi, this is my son, Andy. He has a disability, but he has feelings just like you do, and you've just hurt his feelings.'"

Sepia Levy is an activist, artist, poet, cook, gardener, and cat lover. You need to listen to her closely, or you will miss a lot. Her speech is garbled and hard to understand as a result of cerebral palsy. But that does not stop Sepia from talking. And if you take the time to decode her words, you will learn about the many things she has accomplished in her sixty-eight years.

She was active in the disabilities movement in the sixties, long before the Americans with Disabilities Act of 1990 was passed. In those days people with disabilities were called retarded, crippled, or handicapped and were expected to stay hidden in the closet. But Sepia never liked the closet. She has met five American

presidents: John Kennedy, Lyndon Johnson, Gerald Ford, Jimmy Carter, and Ronald Reagan. She worked to pass state and national legislation that supported the rights of people with disabilities to have jobs, live in the community, and have something to say about their own lives.

Also active in the Civil Rights movement, Sepia says, "I was under the table in a downtown Birmingham store during the riots there—with a black man. We slipped out into an alley and flew away going eighty miles per hour. I was scared all right. I met George Wallace once, during the sixties. He patted me on the top of my head. Can you imagine that? Patting me like I was a family pet. Isn't that an irony—George Wallace being condescending to me. That was before he was in a wheelchair."

Originally from Memphis, Sepia has another claim to fame. With a pleased grin, she says, "Did you know I dated Elvis? We went to the same high school." She says they continued to see each other until she fell in love with Harry, her husband of thirty-five years. Sepia's greatest pride is her long marriage with the man she describes as gorgeous. She likes to talk about her courtship with Harry, who also has cerebral palsy. "We went together three years—back and forth between Birmingham and Memphis, courting by the bus line, airline, and telephone line," she says.

Sepia turns off her television by tapping the remote control with her foot. "My feet are normal, but my hands are not," she says as she slips out of her wheelchair onto the floor, which is where she prefers to sit. Everything in Sepia's home is low so she can reach it from her chair or the floor.

With fire in her eyes and passion in her voice, Sepia talks about what she wants most from other people. "I would like for people to look at me as a human being with a normal brain—not look at me as if I don't understand, can't hear," she offers. "I don't care how much I get up in the world, I'm still looked down on. I'm proud of my life's work. I'm proud of myself and who I am. I've accomplished everything I wanted to. I like myself."

Sepia acknowledges that her strength and determination are the gifts of her heritage. Born into a family of survivors, Sepia explains: "My father came to New York from Russia in 1914. My mother and older brother didn't make it here until 1927—they crossed the Iron Curtain and were caught in Poland. They were locked up there for eight years—ate potato peels to stay alive. My father looked all over the world to find my mother and brother. With the help of a congressman, they were reunited in New York in 1927. I was born after that. I want to live my life well in honor of my parents."

Annie Hull

"Annie's going to walk in the world you and I walk in, not in the world of a handicapped person. So she needs a little bit of an edge." Laura Hull talks about her four-year-old daughter, who has cerebral palsy. "She's so mildly affected that she straddles both worlds. She walks with a limp, and her right arm is weak. But she is not different in our eyes, and I want her to grow up knowing, 'I can do this, I can do that. I can, I can, I can.'

"We don't use the words 'cerebral palsy' around the house. We've never discussed this with Annie's two older brothers. Not long ago I took my seven-year-old son, Matt, to physical therapy with us, and afterwards he said, 'If I walked like Annie could I come to this place too? It's fun.' When Annie gets to kindergarten and has leg braces, she'll have to answer a million questions, so for now I'm focusing on making sure she's happy and likes herself." Annie's days abound with ballet lessons, play groups, and driving her Barbie car. Although somewhat shy and quite attached to her mother, Annie leads an active, fun-filled life.

A devout Catholic, Laura says she believes that there is a reason Annie's involvement is mild. "So many people with cerebral palsy are so severe that they can't advocate for themselves. Maybe she will be able to advocate for others." Not without a sense of humor, Laura adds, "But sometimes I worry about our mother-daughter relationship. That's hard even when you're on equal footing. Think about it—when she finds out she had a stroke in my womb, do you think she's going to be annoyed? God knows, kids blame their mothers for everything anyway!"

Donald Young

Donald Young's piercing blue eyes look directly at you. Within minutes you begin to forget the shock of seeing his scarred face and neck and arms and hands. "Duck," as his friends and family call him, puts you at ease with his quick wit and complete self-acceptance. A slight, trim man with long brown hair sometimes worn in a ponytail on top of his head, Donald talks frankly of the accident that almost took his life at age fourteen. "I was building a fire in the fireplace and threw gasoline on it. It blew up and got me from the waist up," he says softly.

Almost twenty years later, Donald lives a productive and happy life in a small rural Alabama community.

Unable to work full-time, and supported by disability income, he stays busy helping others. His hands are gnarled almost beyond recognition, but he does almost anything he wants with them. As his younger stepson, Matthew, says, "Duck's the man. If he can't fix it, nobody can." In addition to being able to repair whatever is broken, Donald and his fiancée, Sandra, build and paint model race cars. He can do everything except the very detailed painting, which Sandra completes. An avid racing fan, Donald says if he could do anything in the world he wanted, it would be to drive in a NASCAR race.

Donald attributes his life to the care he received at the Shriners Burn Institute for Crippled Children in Cincinnati, Ohio, within five days of the accident. His neighbor, Bryan Sherer, was president of the local Shriners organization at the time Donald was burned. Sherer quickly mobilized the effort to get him treated at a Shriners hospital free of charge, and Donald spent the next ten years of his life traveling back and forth to Cincinnati. He estimates he had close to thirty-five reconstructive surgeries to his face and upper body, with probably as many as fifty total procedures. Pins were placed in his arms and hands to assist in their movement and minimize the affects of contracting and atrophied muscles. The doctors recommended removing several of Donald's fingers, believing they would be useless. Donald resisted the amputations, and only the little finger on his left hand was eventually removed. He says he saw many people coming into the hospital without arms, legs, hands, or feet, and he fought as hard as he could to save his limbs.

Carefully placing a cigarette between two of his overlapping finger stubs, Donald takes a long drag and talks about his life today. "What I want is for people to ask me questions, instead of just staring at me," he says. "Ask anything you want. I'll tell you. I don't think of myself as disabled. I can do just about anything anybody else can, except I can't stay on my feet for a long time. My back has lots of pain. And I can't lift much."

Happy as a boy, Donald says that did not change after his accident. He remembers how his family supported and cared for him during those long years of rehabilitation. Recalling the first time he came home from Cincinnati, when none of his brothers and sisters had seen him yet, Donald says his oldest brother ran to the car. "He didn't even take a second look—he just grabbed me and gave me a hug. My other brothers and sisters were afraid of me, though—afraid they would hurt me. I kept telling them to come on and touch me. Finally I said, 'Okay, I'll go first. I'll hug you, then you hug me back. If you squeeze too hard, I'll let you know.' And that's how they learned to touch me again."

Christina Kuckkahn

Christina Kuckkahn's main discipline problem at her middle school has been that she drives her motorized wheelchair too fast. When the principal was notified, the teachers and school officials made Christina a driver's license. If she speeds, they take the license away and turn off the power to her chair so she has to be pushed. Her mom, Tina, says, "I must confess I drove a motorcycle since I was twelve, so some of that's inherited."

Christina, who has cerebral palsy, is in the ninth grade. During lunchtime in the cafeteria, Christina sits at the end of a table and eats lunch with a group of her friends. They joke, laugh, and flirt with each other, like adolescents do. The girls get shy in front of the camera, and the boys ham it up, asking questions about the equipment, clowning, leaping about, charming, and trying, in general, to get included. Christina joins in the laughter, playing with her ever-present beads.

Christina has an educational assistant named Kim who meets her at school each day. Kim is Christina's bridge-builder, helping her develop age-appropriate friends and activities. Before working with Kim, Christina was pretty dependent. Now she wants Kim to leave her alone with her friends as much as possible. Christina's classmates also help her, particularly Andrew, her boyfriend, who helps her in computer class. One of her friends says, "Christina thinks he's king. She's either totally happy or totally upset. It's a hormone thing."

Tina says she has learned so much from having Christina. One thing is the extent to which her family supports her. The first person in her family to go to college, Tina became a single parent in her sophomore year. "My siblings came forth and said they would raise the child so I could stay in school," she remembers. "Christina gave my life focus and direction when I didn't have any. I graduated summa cum laude from the University of Wisconsin. I was on welfare in college but got a full scholarship to law school."

Christina and Tina belong to Wisconsin's Chippewa Indian Band. Tina, who is active in Native American traditions, says, "Don't limit expectations based on a label. I have done that myself. I feared and grieved when Christina got her chair that she wouldn't be able to join me in our tribal dances. But she did, by just starting to roll her chair back and forth in beat to the music. When we dance in a circle, we consider it a healing circle—that we are praying for her.

"In some cultures a child with a disability is seen as a punishment. For me Christina is a gift from the Creator. Those things that are challenges teach us. I should say 'Thank you for giving me this challenge.'"

Christina and Tina struggle with their relationship, just as most mothers and their adolescent daughters do. Christina can be obstinate, refusing to do anything her mother asks. Tina worries about what will happen to Christina when she is no longer here. She realizes she will be caring for Christina the rest of her life, and the thought terrifies her.

But both mother and daughter are strong. Tina says, "Spirituality is a gift we can all give Christina. She doesn't have to walk. I prayed out loud with her recently and asked her if there was anything she wanted to ask the Creator. Christina said 'Yes,' and I got real excited. Then she said, 'Creator, can I have a purple necklace?'"

Willie James Moore, Jr.

He proudly calls himself the "Deaf Chef." Twenty-eight-year-old Willie James Moore, Jr. loves working at Tracy's Restaurant, where the motto is: "Food from the heart." James says with a grin, "I can show off my cooking skills at Tracy's." James, who was taught to cook as a little boy by his mother, says, "I watched her, then I'd try it on my own. Now I cook a whole lot better than her."

James lost his hearing at age three from a high fever. Hearing aids help a little, and he lip-reads to communicate with hearing people. He loves to play basketball and football with his son, Demetrius. He enjoys road trips, and he loves fishing.

Self-described as easy-going, fun-loving, nature-loving, and kid-loving, James's favorite thing next to cooking is "helping people if they need help, no matter who they are. I like being friends with people. I think when people don't treat me right, it's because they're not used to being around deaf people. If I could change anything, I would teach people sign language so they could communicate more with deaf people."

James says these are the best days of his life, because he has found, in his words, "the most lovable person in the whole world. Jean Ann Stallworth offers me love with honor and trustworthiness and respect. I made a proposal to her and she accepted, and hopefully we can be married before the year 2000." Jean, who is also deaf, has two girls—one who is deaf, and the other hearing. Already planning his and Jean's wedding, James says he might do some of the cooking for the reception. "But not the cake," he says with a big smile. "I'll have a bakery do that. I don't mind cooking, but not on that day, for that crowd."

Michael Raymond

Michael Raymond's message is clear and simple: "I don't like to be called retarded, and I don't like to be called disabled. I want to be called a human being."

Mike stands outside the home he shares with his wife of twenty-six years, but stays inside the fence around his yard. His "watchdog," a cat named Candy, seems to listen while Mike talks about the twenty years he lived in a state institution for people with developmental disabilities.

"I didn't like the way they treated us. They used to put us in straitjackets and stuff like that. I went to school but didn't learn very much. I met my wife there—she lived there too.

Mike was placed in the state institution at two years of age. He was told as a child that his parents were dead and never saw them until after he was married. He says, "My wife and I went looking for my mother on our honeymoon, and we found her. She wasn't dead. We still visit her." Mike's parents, like many at that time, had been advised by his pediatrician to "put him away" and forget he was ever born.

Dressed for work, Mike is about to start a new job as a custodian. He has tried lots of different things, like washing dishes and loading trucks, but he has trouble keeping a job. Sometimes he does not know how far to go when teasing coworkers, and he is easily offended with suggestions for changing his ways. Usually he will just walk away and not come back when things are not going well on the job.

Mike's voice softens when he talks about his nineteen-year-old daughter, who is in college in Milwaukee, studying to be a special education teacher. He becomes tearful as he says, "I'm proud to have my daughter, because I think if you guys can have kids, why can't I? My daughter gets upset when she hears people put us down."

A longtime self-advocate, Mike has accomplished a lot since his years in an institution, not allowing his mild retardation or partial blindness to stop him. He speaks to statewide groups, and lobbies legislators for better laws for people with disabilities. He visits group homes and advises professionals on ways life can be better for people living there.

"I'm the proudest of when I got picked to be the president of Self-Advocates Becoming Empowered (SABE) of Washington," Mike says. "We have four chapters: Bremerton, Port Orchard, Gig Harbor, and Puyallup-Tacoma. We had our convention at the Executive Inn in Fife, and a hundred people were there. We had our own rooms at the hotel.

"I'd like to see people understand what we try to say, and let people know we're out—not to be strange to people—but to do the best job we can. Other people without disabilities, they don't mean any harm against us, and they don't know we have a disability. I've been accused of stuff I didn't do because I look and talk a little different.

"I'm very honored to help you write this book, because we can't help it that we're this way. That's the way God borned us. If I could change anything, I would put handicaps in regular school and show normal people that we can do it. And I would come out and tell these people how I feel: We're just as normal as anybody else."

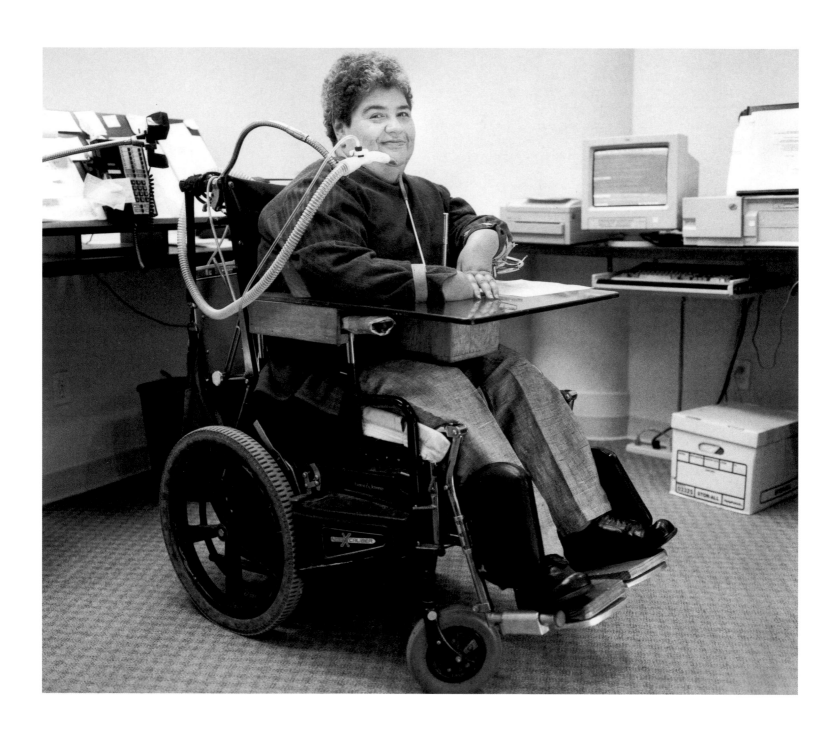

Marilyn Saviola

The co-director of the Center for Independence of the Disabled in New York cannot dress herself, feed herself, go to the bathroom by herself, or breathe without a respirator. Yet she spends eight- to ten-hour days implementing policy, developing programs, writing grants, and speaking to the public—facilitating independence in others with disabilities.

Marilyn Saviola became ill with polio in 1955, when she was ten. In an iron lung for the first six weeks, she has used a respirator to breath since then, and she uses a wheelchair for mobility. Active in getting national disability rights legislation passed, Marilyn says, however, that she does not want to be seen as one-dimensional. "My first identity is not as a working woman with a disability, not as a super-achiever. I'm very driven, but if I weren't disabled, I'd still be driven. My identity includes being a friend, companion, pet owner, political activist, and avid reader. I have a lot of great friends and spend a lot of time with them, both in person and on the phone. I'm not a super-crip or a hero."

With the help of her five personal assistants, who work twelve-hour shifts seven days a week, Marilyn works, travels, enjoys a social life, and advocates for others to do the same. "I'm the proudest of the fact that as of this month I will have been living in the community independently for twenty-five years."

When Marilyn contracted polio, she went to Goldwater Memorial Hospital, a rehabilitation facility in New York City. After being there for a year and a half, she returned home, where her parents lived upstairs and her grandparents lived downstairs.

"It was a completely inaccessible house, and the only time I could get out was when my father carried me," she says. Marilyn was not allowed to go to school because of the ventilator. Instead, the school sent a teacher for an hour and a half three days a week. She says her parents were very supportive of her, but never accepted her disability. "They thought if I only prayed and believed enough in God, this polio would go away," she says.

Marilyn lived at home until she was a teenager, then decided she could not move on with her life in that environment. She went back to Goldwater and helped develop a unit called young adult services, whose primary goal was to help people get out into the community and into independent living. Marilyn completed her undergraduate degree in psychology and her master's degree in rehabilitation counseling while at Goldwater. Then she moved out into her own apartment and worked at Goldwater for eleven years.

"My greatest challenge has been finding the right personal assistants," Marilyn says. "I think the greatest challenge for anyone with a severe disability who needs personal care is getting the right match with the people who are working for you. I had one woman who was with me for twenty-one years before she died. Evelyn has been with me full-time now for eight years, and I love her and the kind of care she gives me.

"My one wish? Well, it's two parts: One is that attitudinal barriers wouldn't exist, and the other is that people would get the services they need—that this would be seen as a right, rather than an entitlement."

Darron Glazier

Watching Brynda gently embrace Darron, their mother, Deb Glazier, chokes back her tears. "It's been so long since she would even come here with me." Darron, thirteen, has mental retardation, seizure disorder, cortical blindness, and cerebral palsy. He cannot speak or walk. Brynda, sixteen, talks about life with her brother. "It was kinda lonely, because I never really talked to him or anything 'til about a month ago. I started being nice to him again. And that made me feel better, but it still hurt that I didn't really have a brother or sister. When he was born, he cried every day, all day. My mom and dad were going nuts, and I was really young, so I just tried to act like nothing was going on."

Brynda eased her pain with alcohol and drugs—starting with Darron's phenobarbital when she was five. Today she says, "If I were talking to someone about having a brother with a disability, I'd say, 'Get ready for your parents to become psychotic. And don't try to escape.'"

Deb talks about the decision to put her son in a group home when he was two. "I said from the beginning that over my dead body is my kid going in an institution. But it got so intense. I finally realized I could not do it, no matter how much energy, how much love."

Darron lives in a beautiful group home at the Allegheny Valley Schools in Pennsylvania, Darron's mother uses alternative treatments as part of his care: aromatherapy, massage, bio-magnetics, polarity therapy, and reflexology. Deb says her faith, B'hai, helps her make sense of his life: "We believe the light is unimpeded; it's just the vehicle that's damaged. One of my students asked me if I could genetically engineer away all handicaps, would I? I said, 'Yes, but we would all be missing something really beautiful, something transcendent.'"

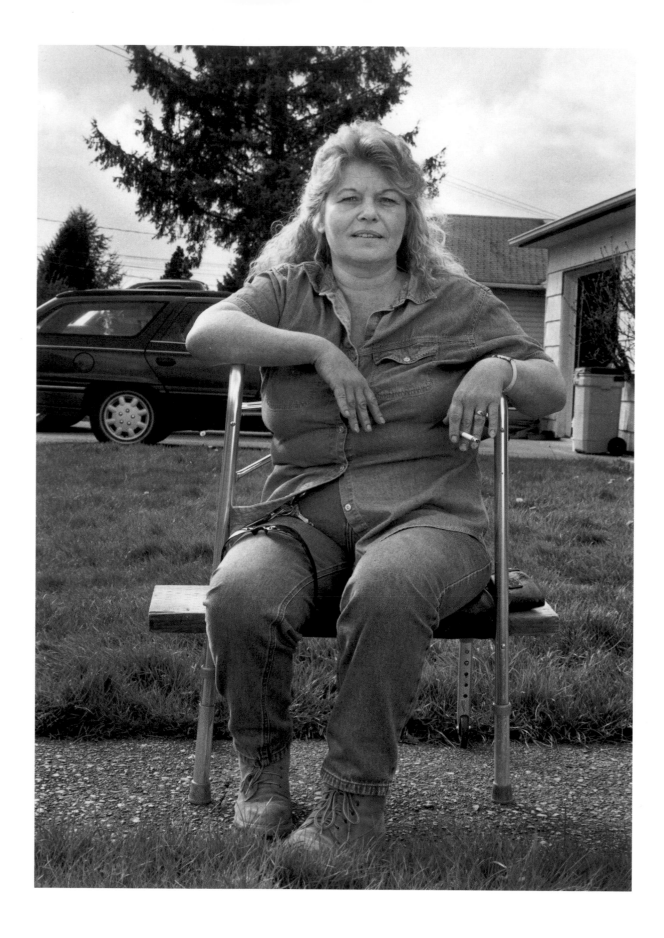

Bunni Barr

"Easter Seals, Bunni. How can I help you?" Bunni Barr, age forty-seven, answers the telephone at the job she loves—receptionist and information specialist with Easter Seals of Washington State. "I worked for twenty years as an executive secretary, then retired and went on disability," Bunni says. "But I didn't earn that check; it just didn't feel right. I sat on my butt at home and watched my soaps. Now I have the perfect job. They could make me president or governor, and I wouldn't change. This is where I belong. I get calls from all over, asking about adaptations, chairs, other equipment. I've been there, I understand what they need."

Bunni was born with cerebral spinal nerve deterioration from feet to jaw, "Although, I never had any trouble talking," she says with a laugh. "My parents were told I would never walk past age ten, but they never told me that. I learned I was 'disabled' at twenty-six, but of course by then I had the mental ability to deal with it. I was told I would never be able to conceive, carry a child, or give birth. I have a daughter and two sons, and three beautiful granddaughters.

"Why is any child told they're disabled? Your child is human, but you don't tell them every day they're human. I realize how lucky I was to have such a positive mom and dad. Otherwise, I don't know where I'd be today. Because of them, I can look at myself and like what I see. Thank you again, Mom and Dad."

Bunni's disease has progressed gradually. For many years she just thought she was uncoordinated and pigeon-toed. "Then I got the diagnosis of cerebral spinal nerve deterioration," she says. "The message leaves the brain correctly but gets crossed up somewhere along the way. I had to learn to deal with doing things differently. We're the most magnificent computer ever made, really, so I keep on trying. If you think about it, you may do something this way, and I may have to do it another way, but I can still get the job done.

"I vowed I'd crawl on the ground before ever using a wheelchair. But in the last few years I've realized how much easier it is for me to do things. When I learned that I could do housework in two hours that had taken me four days to do before, I agreed to the chair."

Bunni lives with one of her sons and her pet iguana, which she calls her watchdog.

She says her children "got it" early about differences, watching the progression of her disease. "They don't hover over me, but they're here if I need them," Bunni says. " They know Mom's too ornery to be fragile.

"You know we are, of course, all very special. However, God knows what we can deal with and gives us all our own disability. I go grocery shopping and look around. Ninety-five percent of the people in the store are more disabled, mentally and emotionally, than I ever thought of being. We all have a disability. It is the ones that are hidden that are the most severe and damaging.

"Sure, I can't run, or walk without canes or a walker, but I'm thankful for being like this. I have been given a special ability to move through life slowly, being able to smell the flowers, to look at things in many different ways and not judge."

"I'm lost from 1979 on back. Once you've had a head injury, it doesn't just come and go. It's with you for life. At times it seems to be gettin' better, but you have to watch the gettin' better, or you'll back-slide."

These are the words of Scott Harper, age thirty-eight, who almost died in a car accident at age nineteen. "Fifteen quaaludes and a fool being a hot rod. And a car. Dodge Charger. It was a good one too. I had it a whole four hours. I was going down the road and I passed out, and my car went on its own toward the gas pumps. Some ladies in a car drove between me and the pumps, to keep me from blowing us all up. At least that's what people told me."

Scott lives alone in a trailer on a dirt road in rural Alabama. There, amid lush woods, it is quiet and peaceful. Scott talks about his memory loss, his poor coordination, and his quick temper.

"Yeah, I had to get out of Birmingham because me and the police didn't get along at all, and I didn't like fighting the police. They didn't put me in jail, but they'd come by my house early in the morning agitatin' me, and heck, I'd just knock hell out of 'em. Wadn't no big deal. Don't come to my house at seven in the morning and expect me to be a perfect gentleman, 'cause I'm not. I don't have to worry about that out here—police don't come out this far very often."

Scott proudly picks up a photograph of the day he received the deed to his trailer. "The National Head Injury Foundation and my mother both helped me get this. I try to live independently. I just sit around and sometimes I drink a beer or two. From what I've understood from all the psychiatrists and psychologists and doctors, I shouldn't be drinking, but you know, that's just something I do—I drink. I listen to country music—especially when LeAnn Rimes is on. I like to walk. I collect Coke stuff, and I'm a big Alabama fan."

Scott's thoughts wander and jump around in his head. He reconstructs his life after his injury. For a time he participated in rehabilitation programs in Birmingham. One program in particular, he says, "gave me all the help I could handle. I was their dishwasher there for nine months. It was fun—I got along with everybody there. Then there was another place where I didn't get along at all. They were too busy trying to tell me about God's way. I know about God's way, but durn, you don't talk about it all the time. Sometimes I get off on this wild goose kick that 'God's Number One and go for God,' and then I get to the point that there is a God, and He looks over us, but God's gonna let us do what we want to do, right or wrong. You can't convert a fool.

"So I don't know about working. I'd like to go back to work, but my attitude sucks. And that's not because of my accident—I was like that before. I try to get along with people, but when I'm working, I cuss a lot, and you don't do that at work. And I have a thing about cigarettes—I smoke a lot.

"I don't know what my problem is. I'm not much on gettin' along with folks no more. I'd like to have my lady friends here, but I won't get into that. I stay lonely. Even when my company comes over, I feel lonely, 'cause being on your own . . . I used to think it was great, but as you get thirty-eight years old, you get to thinking, 'Man, I'm still by myself. I'm alone.'"

Elaine Isemann

Elaine Isemann sits at her kitchen table listening to the birds and drinking her morning coffee. At age forty-seven, she is moving back into her childhood home, after residing in group homes since the age of fifteen. Elaine will be living with her boyfriend of twenty-five years, Peter, and two other people with disabilities.

The only surviving child of her parents, who had three stillborn children, Elaine's development was typical until age four, when she contracted encephalitis from a mosquito bite. Elaine was left with mild mental retardation and spasticity; she now uses a walker to get around, and her speech is labored. Still she holds a job doing contract piecework and enjoys making crafts as well.

In a still somewhat unusual arrangement, Elaine's parents left their home to The ARC of Union County, New Jersey, with the agreement that Elaine could live in it as long as she wishes. The house, newly renovated with public funds, will continue to serve as a home for other adults with disabilities.

Pleased to be home again, Elaine walks around the yard, next door to the same neighbors who lived there when she was a child. Down the street is the church she attended then, and where she met Peter. Today is Fat Tuesday; Elaine decides to give up donuts for Lent. She smiles as she looks across at the wooded lake. It is a beautiful day for a homecoming.

Elaine proudly serves as tour guide for visitors to her house today, and she enjoys pointing out special nooks and crannies her father designed when he built the house nearly fifty years ago. When asked if she and Peter have wedding plans, Elaine stops, waits a minute, and says with a smile, "Oh, no, don't you start that too."

Teresa Case

Teresa Case won't look directly into the camera. She says it is too hard for her to do.

Teresa, who is now forty years old, has lived in an institution for people with developmental disabilities since her early twenties. Years of taking antipsychotic medications have left her stooped, with a shuffling walk, and her eyes dart around nervously. Making eye contact is difficult for Teresa.

Between puffs on a cigarette, Teresa pieces her life together. "I used to be married, a long time ago. But I put it in the paper and got a divorce. He was a colored man. My mother did not like that at all. But I married him anyway. I had a baby boy. He's in his twenties now. I gave him up for adoption. He cried too much."

Teresa is "dually diagnosed" with both a mental illness and a developmental disability. It is hard to know for sure, however, if she really has mental retardation, or if her heavy medication and paranoid schizophrenia just make her appear to be intellectually slow. Teresa used to read well, and was attractive and flirtatious. Little by little her "normal" life seems to be slipping away.

Teresa's job in a nearby town at a sheltered workshop is a challenge for her. She complains of people stealing her food and stepping on her feet, and she curses and cries frequently and easily. Teresa relies on routine for comfort, and her life revolves around going to work, eating, and smoking cigarettes. She goes on an occasional trip to the fair or zoo, and sometimes a concert.

Teresa's bedroom in a house shared with eight to ten other men and women reflects her need for order. It is neatly arranged with matching furniture, floral curtains and bedspread, and her few carefully placed personal belongings. Teresa has one of only two private rooms in the house, with a sign on the door that says: "Please knock before entering." She knows she is lucky, and enjoys the special privilege. With a knowing smile, she says, "A lot of people would like to have my room, wouldn't they?"

For all the order and tidiness in her outside world, Teresa's inner world seems full of chaos. Her thoughts are free flowing and hard to follow. She jumps from anticipating her fortieth birthday to worrying about being in a crowd to wondering when she is going to die. She worries about running out of cigarettes.

In a sudden thoughtful moment, Teresa says, "I wish I had a nice boyfriend though. It's hard to meet men. Nobody wants to take me out. I like tall men, blond guys. My husband was short. I divorced him because he made me shave his head. My friend Wesley has brown hair. I like him for a friend. If he was blond I might marry him.

"I like ol' Elvis," she continues. "But he's gone now. Took too many drugs, killed himself. I don't think he meant to, though. I think it was an accident. He could have had trouble in his marriage or something."

Teresa agreed to be photographed for and featured in this book, but she struggled with the process. She tried smiling and posing, and finally after repeated attempts, she communicated what was real for her—her shyness and inability to look directly at people. "How does a person get to be outgoing, instead of shy like me?"

Teresa vacillates between feeling proud of her looks and worrying that people think she is too fat or that they dislike her hairstyle. She swings quickly from appearing to be comfortable and enjoying herself to being filled with fear or rage over a casual look or passing word.

Anxious to get away, pacing and smoking, Teresa ends the conversation with, "Tell people I'm a nice person. I am a nice person, ain't I?"

Jeff Bannon

Jeff Bannon sits at his computer, using his index finger to activate the EZ Keys word processing program. A former physical education teacher, football player, and college wrestling champion, Jeff, thirty-nine, used to ride his mountain bike twenty-five miles a day to work. He and his wife Jodi hiked, canoed, jogged, and rock-climbed together.

Jeff was diagnosed with Lou Gehrig's disease—amyotrophic lateral sclerosis (ALS)—at thirty-six. He and Jodi had been married five years and were trying to start a family. After testing, they were told they would never have a child—both of them had fertility problems. Six months after Jeff's diagnosis, Jodi got pregnant. Jeff and Jodi call Jeffrey their miracle baby.

Jeff says he began noticing some twitching and weakness in his arms several years before his diagnosis. The weakness gradually spread throughout his body. ALS is a progressive disease of the nerves that causes muscle weakness and wasting, and is ultimately fatal.

Completely immobilized except for slight movement in his left hand, dependent on a ventilator for breathing, with twenty-four-hour nursing care, Jeff reflects on his life with ALS.

The hardest thing about this disability? Jeff says he could give a different answer every day, every hour. It sounds like a poem:

"Not being able to hold my wife and son tops the long list. Not being able to:

play catch with Jeffrey

feel the weight of his little body

wipe away his and his mom's tears

tell them it's going to be okay.

Sitting all day every day, knowing that this is what I will do tomorrow, and the next day

asking for help—for everything

feeling like I don't have much to give

taking three hours to get dressed, two hours to go to bed every night

seeing Jodi exhausted, all the time

missing all the little things like

walks,

movies,

dinner for two,

sitting beside each other,

saying to Jodi, 'Sit down, I will do the dishes.' "

Jodi, a special education teacher, talks about what is hardest for her. "Watching Jeff lose the ability to do everything he loved. Watching him suffer. Wishing he could wrap his arms around me one more time. Missing sleeping in the same bed and feeling him near me. Missing what he would have done with Jeffrey—wrestle with him, carry him on his shoulders, play with him. Missing our privacy."

Jeff says that Jodi and Jeffrey are constant reminders to him to do what he sometimes does not want to do—live. And Jeff has an unshakable faith in God. Along with being a teacher, Jeff also was a counselor for troubled youth, working in a wilderness program, then a Christian counseling center, for several years. Even through the debilitating course of ALS, Jeff continues to "practice what he preaches."

The Bannons are a strong unit. They laugh—together and often. Their deep love for one another nurtures them through the strains of daily life. And hope is ever present. Jeff is taking a newly approved medication thought to slow down the progression of ALS. Jodi says, "Accepting and living with a devastating illness acts as a sifter and puts life in perspective—it filters out nonessential aspects of life and leaves the most precious. Each day is a gift."

Jeff's greatest fear? "Getting worse, and the inevitable end of this disease. The loss of the use of my arms, then my legs, then my lungs. We continue to ask 'How will we make it?' The whisper from God continues to be, 'My grace is sufficient.' It is not so much death itself that I fear. But Jodi and Jeffrey being without me—it is not supposed to be this way.

"How do I want others to relate to me? Without minimizing my disability, I want people to value me as a person, as a man. Just as I am—a mess of hopes and dreams, doubts and fears. My disability does not affect the essence of my humanity, which is beautiful and broken, dignified and depraved. What I need the most is for people to believe I can still give, and to compassionately, but strongly, call me to that."

Kim Sullivan stands outside her apartment, where she lives independently for the first time, determined to lead as normal a life as possible with the realities of epilepsy. Beautiful and healthy aside from the seizures, which are largely controlled by medication, Kim has the same goals as most other young adults. She wants to work, have fun, and eventually get married. "I want to have kids, but I don't know if I can because of the epilepsy," Kim says. I don't want it to hurt them."

Kim is the twenty-eight-year-old daughter of Pat and Jean Sullivan, and the sister of twenty-four-year-old twins, Kelly and Patrick. True to her football family (her dad is the 1971 Heisman Trophy winner), Kim

loves sports and especially enjoys attending football games. At her family's lake house, she swims and rides her WaveRunner. Kim works in a Montessori after-school program, doing what she likes best—taking care of kids. In her leisure time, Kim enjoys concerts and listening to the "oldies," especially country music.

Even with a full and rewarding life, Kim lives with limitations. Being able to drive a car remains an elusive desire. Without being seizure-free for six months, Kim can't obtain a driver's license. Additionally, her coordination is affected by the seizures and by the medications she will always have to take to minimize them.

Jean admires her daughter's determination to live fully. "Even though she has epilepsy, she has not changed her life or the things she wants to do, other than the driving. She continues to work and to go horseback riding, swimming, boating, and to sporting events. Kim hasn't used her epilepsy as an excuse."

The Sullivan family struggles with the balance between respecting Kim's need and desire to be independent, and taking what they see as necessary precautions to prevent her from being hurt. Kim wishes her family would not worry so much. "Sometimes my family gets kind of overprotective," she says. " I don't think they really are, but sometimes it feels that way."

Jean agrees that she and the rest of the family do try to anticipate Kim's falls, which result from her seizures. "She had stitches from a fall at a dance recital, a broken shoulder from a trampoline, and a cut on the forehead from a backward jump into the swimming pool. A few stitches and broken bones never hurt anybody, but we would like to minimize them."

Kim's younger sister Kelly talks about the impact of Kim's seizure disorder on her as a child. "You learn more compassion, more responsibility," she says. You're little, and you're at dance class at school. Your sister has a seizure, and everyone looks at you, like you're supposed to know what to do, and you're only seven. I think it's made me more aware of other people and more sensitive to other people.

"And there's another thing, which I don't exactly know how to say. Not everybody who looks 'normal' is 'normal.' You know, Kim doesn't look like she has a disability, and I think there are pros and cons to that. She's not really treated differently, and that's both good and bad too. Sometimes maybe she should be given a little more slack or patience. Then the checkout lady at the grocery store might understand that it'll take her a little longer to write a check."

Kim's dream of getting married is about to become a reality. She recently became engaged to Chip, whom she met on a trip to Memphis. Both big fans of Elvis, Kim and Chip loved seeing Graceland together. Kim says she feels stronger now that Chip is in her life. "I have learned how to stand up for myself, and I feel safe and protected with Chip," she says. On one of their first dates Kim had a seizure. Chip was calm, and after being sure Kim was okay, took her home. His ease with Kim's seizure disorder goes a long way with her as well as her family. "My life is better than it ever has been," Kim says with a quiet smile.

Judith Heumann

"People ask, 'How can you get around not being able to walk? To see? To hear? How can you live a life having a learning disability or diabetes or psychiatric disability? It alters your life, and therefore you can't be as good as I am, because I'm this specimen of perfection.' The reality is, everybody is different," says Judith Heumann.

As Assistant Secretary for the Office of Special Education and Rehabilitative Services, U. S. Department of Health and Human Services, in Washington, D.C., Judy administers an agency with a $5.5 billion annual budget and a staff of 350 people, managing programs for 49 million Americans with disabilities.

Judy, disabled with polio as a child, speaks passionately about what she would do—if she could—to change people who do not have disabilities. "I'd give them all a brain transplant, so that differences, whatever they may be, would be 'normal.' I don't like it when people say they don't even remember I'm in a wheelchair. Because I do live my life differently. But what they don't recognize is that disability is truly a natural part of life."

Judy lives this belief daily, in her marriage as well as in her work. Her husband, Jorge, was born in Mexico with a birth injury that left him paralyzed from the waist down. "You know we come from different cultural and religious backgrounds," Judy says. "I am Jewish; he is Catholic. And our political views are certainly not always the same. We have some 'spirited' discussions, shall we say. We're both very strong people, so we grow and change together. The ability to forge a meaningful, committed, long-term relationship is so important to me, as to most people. I wish everyone had such a relationship as ours."

Having devoted her professional life to fighting for empowerment for people with disabilities, Judy still feels frustrated. "The hardest part of this effort is the fact that the obvious seems to be difficult to change. There's been enough interaction going on between disabled and nondisabled people. A lot of people just need to get over it," she says.

Judy's office overflows with photographs of her with both dignitaries and regular folks from around the nation and the world. Acknowledgments, plaques, and framed certificates of appreciation testify to her tireless efforts in the disability rights movement. Our interview is interrupted by a call from an adviser about an evening meeting with Newt Gingrich, [former] Speaker of the House of Representatives. Still she gets back to her point. "There's a much larger number of disabled people out and about now than ever before, so I would think the fear factor would come down more quickly than it has." She elaborates that if a person lives long enough the chances are they will be "disabled" in some way or another; therefore, she sees the need for more of a comfort level between disabled and nondisabled people. "Then people who've become disabled could really talk to others about what their concerns are, and have mentors in those who have also been through what they're going through," she concludes.

Judy yearns for even greater strides than those made through the passage of the Americans with Disabilities Act of 1990 and the Individuals with Disabilities Education Act. A strong believer in our government's responsibility to provide equal opportunity for all, she emphasizes, "I think people need to take responsibility for themselves, their families, and their communities, which are growing more diverse daily. People need to look beyond their fears and stereotypes, and decide how they can be a part of making our communities more inclusive for all people, not just for disabled people. To do that we have to really value ourselves, our families, our communities—the community of the world."

Tyler Marson

Tyler Marson loves to ride his bike, watch the cars in his neighborhood, and run. Recently at his elementary school track meet, as classmates shouted, "Tyler, Tyler!" he placed in both the 50-yard and 100-yard dashes.

Tyler, nine, was born with severe autism, which can cause mental retardation, language and speech deficits, and behavioral problems. There is no cure. The best treatment includes closely monitored behavior modification programs, of which he has the best. In addition to attending public school with a one-on-one aide, Tyler has two aides who help care for him at home, so he can live with his parents and younger brother and sister.

"I've always wanted to be a good mother," Beverly Marson says. "More than anything, Tyler has changed my concept of what that is. I've had this fantasy of seeing my children at their college graduation. After the ceremony, all the family goes to a nice restaurant to celebrate the occasion. I've realized that not only will Tyler never go to college, he won't even be able to sit at the restaurant with us. I've also learned that we can't do this alone. When you support Tyler, you support our family. If you take Tyler on a bike ride or help him in Sunday school, it supports him and us.

"In all the traditional ways we communicate, Tyler doesn't," Beverly continues. "But not long ago we were eating dinner, and Tyler kept putting his hands on [his aide] Fred's face, getting his attention. All of us, Dan, Fred, and I were in tears, because we knew that was Tyler's way of communicating his love for Fred. I want Tyler to have an enviable life, which is a life of people loving you and you loving them. That's what makes us rich. I want Tyler to be rich."

Afterword

Photo by Richard Daley

The foundation of a work of art, which acts as a bridge between the artist and the audience, is built upon our commonly shared humanity, and further, it is this "being human" that gives artistic enlightenment its value. Through art, we expand our understanding of life, of those we may not meet, of a diversity of human dramas in which we may never personally participate. Thus, it is the aesthetic experience that can add a richer complexity to what is, for each of us, a finite journey through life. A book such as *Just As I Am: Americans with Disabilities* offers new insights into a world often outside our own experiences, and yet a world we all share. In this book, all of the individuals struggle to make something of their lives, to take the risks that make life worth the journey. These are true and intimate portraits of Americans with disabilities.

Through the photographs and prose, we become better educated about a subject that for many is both unfamiliar and, possibly, uncomfortable. *Just As I Am* was created by two women who are friends, artists, and professionals working in the field of rehabilitation. The work offers a rare glimpse into the lives of people throughout this country, many with severe emotional and physical disabilities.

These individuals accept themselves for who they are and take pride in what they have and will achieve.

Through these photographs and accompanying text, the reader has an opportunity for thoughtful examination and new understandings. Ellen Dossett faithfully transcribed first-hand commentaries, and through her professionally trained observations, she has crystallized the comments, focusing each story in the way the person wished to be represented. All were asked about their strengths and their heart's desires, and about how they wanted people without disabilities to relate to them. After asking these tough questions and tuning in to the powerful responses, Dossett, as a journalist, then turned to the formidable challenge of sculpting volumes of information into intimate and real literary portraits. She did so boldy and beautifully. And now she graciously invites us to meet the many unforgettable people who invited her in.

Thanks to Carolyn Sherer's black-and-white portraits, we get to know them in another way. Her images are straightforward and honest. The comfort and respect between the photographer and those photographed radiate throughout. Knowingly, the individuals opened themselves to close scrutiny and possible judgment. Because Sherer chose to place the participants in their familiar environments, using only ambient light, the resulting photographs offer the viewer greater insight into their lives—just as they are—without embellishment. Seeing them through the artist's lens, we are privy to their most private thoughts, their vulnerabilities, and their strengths. In the mode of earlier women artists, such as the celebrated Lisette Model and Diane Arbus, Sherer uses the photograph to prolong a unique, intimate moment, one generously shared with us. In contrast to those who came before, Sherer's compositions are empathetic, filled with all the complexities of each individual life and brimming with their courage.

If courage is an inner strength that we each must learn, then this book is a testament to those who have learned well. Sherer and Dossett chronicle what these Americans with disabilities—with odds that at times seem insurmountable—have achieved. Clearly, by drawing from these unique portraits and stories, we enable ourselves to cross the bridge from art to a greater understanding of humanity—to learn, to grow, and to overcome our own prejudices and adversities. And to, indeed, acknowledge our kinship with others, no matter how alike or different from us they are.

RUTH STEVENS APPELHOF, PH.D.
Independent Museum Professional

Resources

AMYOTROPHIC LATERAL SCLEROSIS OR
"LOU GEHRIG'S DISEASE"
Amyotrophic Lateral Sclerosis Association (ALSA)
27001 Agoura Road, Suite 150
Calabasas Hills, CA 91301-5104
800/782-4747

ANENCEPHALY
March of Dimes Birth Defects Foundation (MOD)
1275 Mamaroneck Avenue
White Plains, NY 10605
914/428-7100

ANGELMAN SYNDROME
National Institute of Neurological Disorders
and Stroke
P.O. Box 5801
Bethesda, MD 20824
301/496-5751

ATTENTION-DEFICIT/HYPERACTIVITY DISORDER
The Feingold Association of the United States (FAUS)
P.O. Box 6550
Alexandria, VA 22306
800/321-FAUS

AUTISM
Autism Society of America (ASA)
7910 Woodmont Avenue, #300
Bethesda, MD 20814-3015
800/3-Autism or 301/657-0881

BLINDNESS
American Council of the Blind
1155 15th Street NW, Suite 720
Washington, DC 20005
202/467-5081

BURNS/BIRTH DEFECTS
Shriners Hospitals for Children
12502 N. Pine Drive
Tampa, FL 33612
813/972-2250

CEREBRAL PALSY (CP)
United Cerebral Palsy Associations, Inc. (UCPA)
1660 L Street NW, Suite 700
Washington, DC 20036-5602
800/USA-5UCP

CYTOMEGALOVIRUS (CMV)
National Institute of Neurological Diseases
and Strokes
P.O. Box 5801
Bethesda, MD 20824
301/496-5751

DERMATOMYOSITIS
Myositis Association of America
755 Cantrell Avenue, Suite C
Harrisonburg, VA 22801
800/821-7356

DOWN SYNDROME
National Down Syndrome Society (NDSS)
666 Broadway, Suite 810
New York, NY 10012
800/221-4602

ENCEPHALITIS
National Institute of Neurological Diseases
and Strokes
P.O. Box 5801
Bethesda, MD 20824
301/496-5751

FRIEDREICH'S ATAXIA
National Ataxia Foundation (NAF)
2600 Fernbrook Lane, Suite 119
Minneapolis, MN 55447
612/553-0020

HEARING IMPAIRED
National Association of the Deaf
814 Thayer Avenue, Suite 250
Silver Springs, MD 20910
301/587-1788

MENTAL RETARDATION
The ARC of the United States
500 East Border Street, Suite 300
Arlington, TX 76010
800/433-5255 or 817/261-6003

MISSING LIMBS/AMPUTATIONS
American Orthotic and Prosthetic Association
1650 King Street, Suite 500
Alexandria, VA 22314
703/836-7116

MULTIPLE PERSONALITY DISORDER
International Society for the Study of Dissociation
60 Revere Drive, Suite 500
Northbrook, IL 60062
847/480-0899

MULTIPLE SCLEROSIS
National Multiple Sclerosis Society
733 Third Avenue, 6th Floor
New York, NY 10017-3288
212/986-3240

PHYSICAL DISABILITY
The Lakeshore Foundation
3800 Ridgeway Drive
Birmingham, AL 35209
205/868-2303
www.lkshore.org

POLIO
International Polio Network (IPN)
4207 Lindell Boulevard, #110
Saint Louis, MO 63108-2915
314/534-0475

PRADER-WILLI SYNDROME
Prader-Willi Syndrome Association
5700 Midnight Pass Road, Suite 6
Sarasota, FL 34242
800/926-4797

PROXIMAL FEMORAL FOCAL DEFICIENCY (PFFD)
March of Dimes Birth Defects Foundation (MOD)
1275 Mamaroneck Avenue
White Plains, NY 10605
914/428-7100

RETINOBLASTOMA
American Association of the Deaf and Blind
814 Thayer Avenue, Suite 205
Silver Spring, MD 20910
301/588-6545

SCHIZOPHRENIA
National Mental Health Association (NMHA)
1021 Prince Street
Alexandria, VA 22314-2971
800/969-NMHA

SEIZURE DISORDER
Epilepsy Foundation of America
4351 Garden City Drive, Suite 406
Landover, MD 20785
800/332-1000
www.EFA.org

SPINA BIFIDA
Spina Bifida Association of America (SBAA)
4590 MacArthur Boulevard NW., Suite 250
Washington, DC 20007-4226
800/621-3141
www.SBAA.org

SPINAL CORD INJURY
National Spinal Cord Injury Association
Zalco Building
8701 Georgia Avenue, Suite 500
Silver Spring, MD 20910
800/962-9629

SPINAL MUSCULAR ATROPHY (SMA)
Rehabilitation Research and Training Center in
Neuromuscular Diseases
RTC: Rehabilitation in Neuromuscular Diseases
MED: PM and R
University of California
Davis, CA 95616-8655
530/752-2903

STROKE
National Stroke Association
96 Inverness Drive E., #1
Englewood, CO 80112
303/649-9299

TRAUMATIC BRAIN INJURY
Brain Injury Association, Inc.
105 N. Alfred Street
Alexandria, VA 22314
800/444-6443

VATER ASSOCIATION
VATER Association
520 Greensboro Street
Starkville, MS 39759
601/323-1951

LAKESHORE FOUNDATION

205/868-2303 www.lkshore.org

Since 1984, the Lakeshore Foundation has been a leader in providing opportunities for children and adults with physical disabilities to excel in all aspects of community life including sports, recreation, work, worship, education and more. The Foundation is the only organization in Alabama, and one of but a few in the United States, providing a full range of quality of life programs for people with physical disabilities.

We serve people with a variety of conditions that restrict activities of daily living and work including, but not limited to, spinal cord injury, amputation, head injury, stroke, multiple sclerosis, arthritis, cerebral palsy, post-polio and spina bifida.

Our programs provide opportunities to maximize quality of life, pursue individual interests, and maintain an active lifestyle. We bring together a unique combination of personnel, facilities, equipment, and support for both newly disabled persons and those who have lived with disability for some time.

Lakeshore Foundation's participation in the development of *Just As I Am: Americans with Disabilities*, from its community service photographic exhibit phase through the completion of this book, exemplifies our commitment to the active participation of people with disabilities in the life of their community.

 CIVITAN INTERNATIONAL
RESEARCH CENTER

This book is not just a book. It is a tribute to human creativity, collaborations, vision, and determination. *Just as I Am: Americans with Disabilities* began as a wild idea with a straightforward premise. The idea was that we find a way to celebrate the remarkable human spirit as expressed in the lives of Americans with diverse challenges and life circumstances—which collectively are labeled as "disabilities." The premise was that this project could be launched with the help of our friends, the newly funded AmeriCorps Program here at our Civitan International Research Center, the talented leadership of Dr. Ellen Dossett, and the volunteer contribution of the photographer, Carolyn Sherer—and that there would be many audiences with whom to share these portraits.

We are exceptionally proud of this product—a magnificent book that speaks to the heart, mind, and soul of humankind. Our center's mission is to enhance the quality of life for individuals and families affected by developmental disabilities. We strive to realize this mission through research, interdisciplinary training, exemplary clinical and community services, technical assistance, and information dissemination. This book is an innovative way to share what we have learned—and what others have learned through their own life experiences. We thank everyone who made this project the undeniable success it is. Above all, we thank the individuals who so eloquently share their stories on these pages.

With great pride and gratitude,

SHARON LANDESMAN RAMEY, PH.D.
CRAIG T. RAMEY, PH.D.
DIRECTORS OF THE CIVITAN INTERNATIONAL RESEARCH CENTER
UNIVERSITY OF ALABAMA AT BIRMINGHAM

The University of Alabama at Birmingham's Human Resource Management Department has a long history of working with people who have disabilities and are seeking employment. The department also supports current employees whose lives are changed by injury or disease. The cooperation and innovations of faculty such as Dr. Ellen Dossett and Ms. Carolyn Sherer have been invaluable in these efforts.

It is our hope that all employers, after reading *Just As I Am*, will broaden the view of what inclusion means.

OFFICE OF HUMAN RESOURCE MANAGEMENT
UNIVERSITY OF ALABAMA AT BIRMINGHAM